M000312627

In His Footsteps

How to be happy soul-deep

Margaret Agard
Parker Wentworth Publishing

IN HIS FOOTSTEPS:
How to be happy soul-deep

Published by Parker Wentworth Publishing
First Printing 2010
© 2010 by Margaret Agard

Cover design by Tudor Maier, www.tudormaier.com
Cover illustration of The Good Shepherd © Greg Olsen
By arrangement with Greg Olsen Art Publishing Inc.
1-208-888-2585 www.gregolsen.com

All Biblical quotes are from the Authorized King James Version
(KJV)

Published in the United States by Parker Wentworth Publishing
Printed in the United States

For information:
PARKER WENTWORTH PUBLISHING
PO BOX 173 DUCK WV 25063

International Standard Book Number:
13 digit ISBN 978-0-9767327-4-7
10 digit ISBN 0-9767327-4-2

Library of Congress Control Number: 2010931210

Dedication

To my husband Parker
whose eyes reflect a life
of generosity and love

Table of Contents

Introduction

One day I just picked up my pen—or in this case my keyboard—and started writing my daily life, the way you might share it with a friend or neighbor. Except from a deeper place.—the place where I talk with God.

I wrote about what it's like to struggle—to struggle with the daily challenges of work, raising teenagers, stressing over money, and feeling prompted to reach out and help others, but being so overloaded with things to do already that I couldn't see how to do even one more thing.

I struggled to submit my will to God's and to follow His leadings and promptings. He never demanded. Just requested. Or when I'd asked about what to do about a problem often He'd actually tell me what to do and then waited to see what I would do. Every time I followed His will, counsel, or prompting, I was filled with joy and happiness—soul-deep happiness.

But time and again, I refused to follow. It just seemed too hard. When I did it, my days of submission were both simpler and more fulfilling. I was filled with energy. I was never discouraged or stressed. At the end of each day, I felt deep satisfaction and pleasure. I had true purpose to my actions, even the simplest ones. I knew—because people told me so—that my simple actions, such as bringing a dinner, making a telephone call, or apologizing, were making a difference. When I listened, my life had meaning.

And yet it continued to be a struggle. Isn't that strange? I was just too busy, too afraid, too offended. It was as if I was saying to God, "Let me live my selfish life in misery and anxiety. I don't have time to be happy."

It was my own personal "Groundhog Day" experience, the movie where Bill Murray keeps reliving the same day over and over. That was me then. Even now when I stray— because who doesn't—it still is me. God asked me to do a particular thing (help, forgive, move, trust more, or give up an activity.) I

11

didn't want to. I argued, ignored Him, found other things to do, tried a different way. Finally I did it. When I did, I was happy. My problems were handled, often miraculously. God asked me to do something else. I didn't want to. Repeat, repeat, repeat.

Until at last I got it: The struggle was between what I thought would make me happy and what God knew would make me happy. I'm his child. He knows me better than I know myself. Counseling with and following God's promptings is what it takes to be happy. It's not about waiting until I have my life in order so I have time, money and energy to listen to God and do what He wants. It's about listening to God, doing as He asks, and then He gets my life in order. What a gift.

That's what this book is about. What God wants for me and wants for you, too—to learn how to be happy. All the rest of it— the simpler life, the true purpose, the energy, the joy, the focus— come along as part of the package, the life of soul-deep happiness.

The Yellow Pad: A Wisdom Prayer
April 8th

God gave me a gift today. Awhile ago I gave up trying to make my life work with all my lists, calendars and yellow sticky notes and just said, "God, I need help! I have clients who are expecting custom reports, EPA global warming scenarios to run, church members who need me—the Relief Society president— to come and help with emergencies, two sons who need rides for school and doctor appointments, and a husband who wants my full attention. No matter what I do, there's a longer list that doesn't get done."

The list on the yellow pad gets longer and longer and I sleep less and less. I tell my kids, my clients, and my Relief Society counselors that if it's not on the yellow pad, then it's not getting done, so make sure you see me write it there. Even then, it might not get done.

Now it's in God's hands. Each day I get up, take my legal-sized, yellow pad with five pages of unfinished to-do's (one on each line) and make my list of priorities for the day on another sheet. Then I take that sheet and pray and ask God what He wants me to do. Most of the time, I cross off half of my list and then add two or three people He wants me to call.

Lately I haven't even looked at the yellow pad except to add things then asked God each day what my tasks are. I'm afraid to look at the pad. I don't want to know what I'm forgetting. Today as I listed my to-do's for the day—finish the income taxes, take Ryan to the doctor, have the missionaries to dinner, <u>make</u> the dinner first—I could feel the Spirit whispering, "Look at the yellow pad. Look at the yellow pad."

I said, *I don't want to look at the yellow pad. It discourages me to see the yellow pad.*

Finally, at 10:00 this morning, when the Spirit still hadn't given up, I said, *Fine. You win. I'll look at the yellow pad. There must be an important task I'm overlooking.*

I looked through all five pages, searching for that important task, crossing off the things I've already done as I searched and, guess what. There's nothing left to be done on the yellow pad.

How did God do that?

The Room
April 9th

I wake thinking of The Room. I know I'm going to be back there again before my years of serving as Relief Society president are over, and I both dread and desire it. Being in That Room confronts me with people's deepest sorrows and most profound joys. I witness these and feel my own. That is The Room. Wherever pain cries out for comfort, hope and help.

The first time I go to The Room is less than a month after I've been called and set apart as the Relief Society president. While visiting people in the local community hospital friends discovered an 83-year-old woman who is a member. She isn't attending church because for the entire year she's lived in our area her husband has been dying. We didn't know of her as she hadn't had her church records transferred from her former home hundreds of miles away.

Now, he is in the hospital in the final stages of death, her family is far away and his family is angry with her. She needs help and support, I am the Relief Society president—so I go.

I find her in the clinic of the hospital having her own illnesses treated. I tell her who I am—my name of course—but mostly my calling. She knows what it means to be the Relief Society president because she looks frantically into my eyes for the peace she is searching for, pulls me down beside her and begins to talk, her words spelling out her pain and troubles. Then she asks the question. "Why is God doing this to me? Why? I've lived a good life. This is painful. Why me? Why now?"

Ah, now I see. It isn't The Room. It is the Question.

The Question I am asked so often. The Question I have asked so often. She is just one of many I am to meet in the coming months asking this question in many different-but-somehow-the-same rooms. The handbook for Relief Society presidents is direct and straightforward. Even if I know the answer to the Question, I am not to share it. This is her struggle, her time for growth. This is a relief, because most of the time, I don't know the answer. And when I think I do, I'm often wrong. The answers aren't always what we think. But the pain is clear.

And so, I sit in the room, feeling the pain our choices bring. And the pain that living life gives us. Because that is the gift given to the Relief Society president, to feel others' pain on the deepest level.

I pray before I go to each Room, each struggling sister and immediately the Spirit is there and I feel God's presence. I sit, and feel, and say nothing but the words I am given to speak. They are seldom words of advice, and always words of comfort. *God loves you. He hears you. Turn to Him. He will comfort you. Only He can heal this pain.*

I feel the pain and, after three months of being Relief Society president, I spend an entire afternoon just weeping. I know now why He was called Man of Sorrows. I am walking hand in hand with the Master as part of this calling.

It is only when I turn away, and go back to real life and phone calls, and making doctor's appointments that the Spirit slowly subsides. It's then I often think, *Can't she see how she caused this?* At times we are the cause of our own pain. But I don't ask those questions while I am there with the Master beside me. Then, I only feel His love and peace. His desire to use me as the physical instrument for His children, for His daughters, to feel that love and peace coming from me. A few think it is me. But the wise know it is Him.

I am to give no answers, but only to direct them to Him. When they go to Him, I see the change. It will be all right. They are not alone. The pain is there, but it is less, and hope is there, too. Those who turn to Him struggle, but eventually they figure it out. It hurts less when I serve others. When I forgive, the anger, hurt and fear I'm holding on to go away and I am at peace. I am free.

This is also the gift of the Relief Society president. To see the growth of others and to feel the love of God. I weep once again—this time with tears of joy at the nobleness of my brothers and sisters here on earth. At the calm acceptance of trouble and suffering as they rise above it to serve others, to forgive things that seem impossible to me to forgive.

For those who refuse to turn to Him, I am there. Still listening, still comforting, still bringing soup and offering rides and firewood, and hoping and praying they will take the greater gift—the love God has for them.

Meeting Parker
April 10th

A few years after my first marriage of twenty five years ended when my then husband, father of our eight children, went to live the life of a gay artist, I met my now husband, Parker, over the Internet.

What I was really trying to do was to keep my oldest son Michael from going 2000 miles away to a university to finish his Bachelors degree and find a wife. Finishing his degree wasn't the issue. Nor was finding a wife – except for the part about going far away

"Nooooo," I wailed at him. "Don't go there. You'll marry some girl from California and then you'll have to live near HER family and we'll never see you again."

Look at this I told him pointing to a new singles match-up site just for church people. This was 1997 before these sites were everywhere and for every kind of interest.

You can meet someone from here I told him. Then I coached him on how to fill out the form. Tell the truth I told him. There's a lid for every pot as my brother Jim says. Be exactly who you are so you'll meet the person who will love you just as you are.

Rather than fill out his profile - although I'm controlling enough to do that - I set the example by filling out one for myself. I wrote about my eight children and mentioned that I loved children but didn't want any more and these were almost all grown – just two left in high school. Then I mentioned my job as an executive in the high tech industry. Thinking I might attract another executive type – and they like to golf- I decided to make it clear I hate golf. In fact, I wrote, I'd rather give birth again than play golf.

A day or so later I got an email from Parker who also hates golf. A match made in heaven.

The upshot? Michael did go far away where he met and married Mendy whose family lives just a couple hours away from our Virginia home. I married Parker and moved from urban DC to 10 acres in rural California.

See? God does have a sense of irony.

An Angry Family Home Evening
April 11th

Matthias, my youngest son, turned another family home evening into an angry blast-against-God again last night. "I hate God. He sucks. I'm not asking for everything, but couldn't God give me a break once in while?" Matthias is 18, a senior, and is studying the Old Testament in early morning scripture study this year, so he has lots of ammunition for his belief that God is as an angry, vengeful, jealous Being.

"The good people suffer the most," says Matthias, "While the people who don't go to church get everything."

"All what everything," I ask. "Peace, joy, love, comfort?"

Matthias hates it when I talk like this, but I'm getting a little tired of his griping, so I just cut to the heart of it.

Off he goes, "Good people go to church in rags while

people who don't go to church have nice clothes, and good cars and big houses."

He's pushing it now. "Who do you know who goes to church in rags? Anyway, having money and nice cars doesn't mean you don't suffer and have pain. Everyone does. It's why we're down here. To grow. You might as well accept it now or go through your entire life bitter and complaining. You can't grow without any suffering. No pain, no gain, right?" As a weight lifter, he's heard that analogy from me so many times I don't need to go any further.

"Yeah. That, too. He sent us down here knowing we're going to have pain. What kind of loving God is that?"

"One who loves us enough to let us grow," I say.

"He even knows we're going to fail. God tells us we're going to fail. He knows it and sent us down here anyway. Then lords it over us, telling us he's perfect and he's so great and he'll take care of it for us," says Matthias.

This is a new twist on an old argument. I have to think for a moment about this one. Matthias's the last of my eight children going through the teenage years. I've usually heard it all before, so I can't help but admire him for thinking of it. And I'm kind of grateful, too. After 18 years of the same discussions—the names change, the arguments stay the same—it's nice to hear a new one.

I say, "God knows what you're capable of. It's like becoming an Olympic skater. You can't become a world class ice skater without falling. God says to get up and try again, you'll get it. Most of us have been working on the same things for 20 years, and we're still falling. But if He hasn't given up, why should we? He even says, 'I'll show you how it's done.' He's not showing off. He knows we have what it takes and He wants us to get there.

He says, 'Take my hand. I'll help you the first couple of times. You'll get the hang of it, and I'll forget that you fell. So should you.' How does this make him a terrible God?"

His face is still bitter.

I am getting a little tired of this anger and tension and say, "Matthias. Just drop it. These arguments get us nowhere. You keep saying the same things. I can't change your mind. And anger doesn't help. I don't mind questions, but you aren't questioning—you're just complaining."

He says, "This is how I ask questions."

"Then take this one to God, because only He can answer this in a way you'll understand."

Matthias says, "I did ask Him."

A moment of silence. This is good news. I ask, "What did He say?"

Matthias says, "He said look around you at all you do have."

I almost laugh as hope wells up in my heart. I know for sure Matthias is praying and God is answering his prayers, because that is the answer. But he still sounds bitter and sarcastic. A lot of us get the answers and then ignore them, and I worry this is what is happening with Matthias.

I say, "Well, then do that, because that's what works."

He's offended. "I do do that. I always thank him when I pray. And my car is still broken and my life still sucks. No offense, but I have to live here with you and my stepdad and not back East with my friends. My friend Martin's parents gave him a car and everything else, and they don't go to church."

I say, "They just gave him a car, and Martin is a happy boy?"

Matthias says, "No, he's not. He's an idiot. He crashed his car, and he flunked out of school, and he's on drugs, and they told him when he's 18 that he's out of the house. And he'll really be in trouble then, because he doesn't know how to work or how much anything is worth."

I say, "Why is that?"

He says, "Because his parents gave him everything. He didn't have to work for any of it, and he isn't even grateful."

Matthias and I just look at each other for a moment and then I say, "Son, I think you just answered your own question."

Peacocks as Watchdogs? Think Again
April 14th

Peacocks are beautiful birds, and they make good watch-dogs, which is why we have them. Or so my husband, Parker, says. Parker just loves animals and adventure and oddities. That's really why we have peacocks—and emus and a llama and a donkey. If you haven't heard them before, peacocks scream like fighting cats in heat, only harsher and louder. A friend played his bagpipes on our property one day, and the peacocks started screaming. They were louder than the bagpipes! Parker says if they weren't so beautiful they'd be extinct just because of that sound. I agree wholeheartedly.

For the last two weeks various animals have come near—not on—the property, setting off the peacocks around three or four in the morning. First it was coyotes who set up a little coyote-peacock chorus with the peacocks. Then it was male turkeys whose loud gobbles used to bother me, but thanks to the peacocks, they sound soft and gentle to me now. Then it was the dog that belongs to the people who live on the opposite hill. The dog, scared by the peacocks' screams, started barking, and the peacocks screamed at each bark. That went on for an hour. Then the alarm went off.

One night, we didn't have a clue what set them off. Parker said it was probably a raccoon nosing around the chicken pen or the garden.

About 5:30 every morning the peacocks fly up to the deck outside our second story bedroom and stomp around. They go from there to the roof. It sounds like a two-hundred-pound man up there stomping around. It was scary at first because I thought maybe there was a two-hundred-pound man stomping around up there, but then I realized it was the peacocks.

See where we are? A two-hundred-pound man could come onto our property setting off the peacocks (that we would think were screaming at a raccoon) then climb up on our deck to force his way in - even stomp around on the deck - and we would ignore him, thinking it was just a peacock. So much for the peacocks-as-watchdogs theory.

When a Child Forgives You
April 16th

Daniel, my 20-year-old son, came in and lay down on the bed next to me last night to chat. He told me he was sorry about his rebellions, and all the trouble he caused for his stepdad. He needed to say it, and I was glad to hear it. But he didn't *have* to say it. I knew he would come to this eventually, because he's a good young man.

So this is for those of my eight children who haven't reached that point yet. If I should die before you reach that point, then don't worry that you didn't get to tell me before I died. I knew you'd get here eventually.

But, especially, let me say thank you for forgiving me my failures and mistakes enough to see me as worth apologizing to. That's what it takes before you ask me for forgiveness - forgiving me first. And I do appreciate it. So even if you never said it while I was alive, it's ok. Although, it is nice to hear it.

My eldest son, Michael, once told me he'd figured out that I was the perfect mother for him. I asked why, and he said it was because he was kind of an odd person with a sarcastic sense of humor and I appreciated his humor. I asked if he didn't think I'd warped him into that, and he said no. He was just that way. Also, the best part of my mothering is that I was never very compassionate. Well true but who thinks of that as a good character trait?

I asked what he meant by that. Was he talking about how I used to tell them not to bleed on the carpet?

No, he said he's a bit of a whiner and a complainer. He recognizes that but says I never fell for it. Basically just told him to man up and get on with life.

Hearing the Spirit
April 17th

When I was about 23 years old, I heard a person in church talk about her conversations with God. Conversations? I didn't know it was possible. I just thought you prayed, got up, went about your day, and things either happened or they didn't.

I went to the Lord and said I would like to have experiences that helped me understand when He was talking with me. It seemed illogical that He could, since if I hadn't been able to understand yet, what could He do differently? But you never know with God. He's accomplished bigger miracles. It doesn't hurt to ask.

The next day, I made a pot of chili that kept getting bigger and bigger. I had this recurring thought that I should invite a particular couple—let's call them the Joneses—to dinner. I kept trying to dismiss it, to argue with it.

They just came on Friday. They'll think it's weird to get another invite so soon.

"Invite them anyway," said the little voice in my head.

Tonight's family home evening night—we're only supposed to have family.

"Invite them to stay for family home evening."

Finally, I thought, OK. *I'll invite them.*

I did, and they were pleased. They came and ate. Sat through family home evening, which was a lesson and activity on tithing.

As the lesson ended they said, "We haven't paid our tithing in a while. We were committed to paying all we owed. For various reasons our paycheck was short, and we had just enough money come in on Saturday to pay only our tithing. We're about out of food and we would have no food money. So we spent all Saturday deciding what to do. On Sunday we just handed in our check to pay our full tithing and trusted in the Lord to provide. By the end of Church on Sunday, we had invitations to dinner every night except tonight. Then this morning you called."

I had three more experiences like that in a week. Every time, I argued with the thought. Every time when I finally listened and acted, I discovered the people had been praying for that exact thing. I cannot describe the joy I felt being an instrument in the Lord's hand, helping people's faith to grow.

From that, I learned to recognize the Lord's prompting. It is a still, small voice- no more than a thought. I learned that if I'm arguing with a thought and it keeps coming back, it's Him. I don't argue with myself.

I learned we are often each other's answers to prayers. I understand now why we are told that the Lord will hold us accountable for the good we might have done, had we done our duty.

I've learned that if I'm praying and thinking about a concern, certain Scriptures just jump out at me. That's the Spirit. But I have to be reading the scriptures. Other times, as I write in my journal about my questions, certain thoughts come to me. As I write them, I recognize them as being of the Lord. But I have to be writing in my journal.

And the most wonderful gift of all is to be able to pray with my husband until we come to a unity of the spirit, for then I am assured this is of the Lord.

Whenever I ignore the Voice, I regret it. The Lord wants to bless me. I frequently make it impossible for Him to do that, especially when it doesn't look like a blessing at first. Once I learned to recognize the spirit, I had to learn to truly trust God and act on the prompting because, often, it is after the show of faith that the blessings come.

One time I sensed a year in advance that I was going to get a job offer and that I should take it and move to a city 2,000 miles from our current home. Three of the children were in high school and very happy where we were living. Michael was just finishing his black belt in karate and loved his class and his friends. We spent a year praying about it as a family and preparing. Looking back on it, different children have told me they are glad now that we moved. Their lives would have been much different if we'd stayed where we were. In the new place they met people of many different cultures and backgrounds. This helped them become more open and accepting of others. The new school put a heavy emphasis on preparing for college rather than technical training. The near-by city gave them experiences not possible in our former midwestern community. They had the best of both available to them.

But it was not painless. The first year after the move was horrible. The three older children struggled the most. Elisabeth did not come out of her room for a year except to go to school. Michael was so angry, he failed all of his classes or came close to it (while scoring 1400 on the SATs). Christian had emotional scars he worked for years to overcome. The only thing that kept us from moving right back was the knowledge that this was of the Lord and the growing pains would be worth it.

Then suddenly the worst was over. New friends, new experiences, new attitudes brought happiness.

I had the gift of visiting my father often during the last six months before he died. I sat next to him with my brothers and sisters as he drew his last breaths. As painful as it was, it would have been more painful to not be there.

I learned from all those experiences. I learned that the longer the notice is that the Lord gives me for an impending change and the stronger the prompting, the harder it is going to be. But the joy is always as great as the pain. Michael and Flora have both returned to that neighborhood we left. They both said they are glad now that we moved.

I think He gives me that extra time and prompting as a blessing so that I can be assured I'm on the right path when all seems to my limited view to be going wrong.

The first step is learning to recognize that spiritual prompting and then trusting enough to act on it.

Preparing to Die
April 18th

A year ago, I had this sense that I would die this year in the spring. Spring officially ends on June 20. Because of my own personal beliefs, I took this to be the truth. While readers of this entry might not have the same beliefs, there might be a similar experience you would believe. Perhaps a doctor saying you have cancer throughout your body.

This is what I did. I immediately made lists of things to do: Finish the will. Talk with the children. Clean my house. Lose weight. (Parker asked, "Why do you want to lose weight if you are going to die?" To which I answered, "So I won't be heavy in my coffin.") Start a journal of the last year. Get the book <u>On Death and Dying</u> by Elizabeth Kubler Ross and re-read it. And on and on.

Then I thought, *What am I doing? When confronted with life's most profound and frightening change, I am just acting like me. I haven't suddenly become a sensitive, people person who stops to smell the roses. I'm still just an organized, take-care-of-the-practical-details list maker.*

Later, I started thinking about how I'd like to live my last year. I realized I wanted to keep doing what I was doing—only more of some things and less of others. I love my life.

I read a short anecdote about a student approaching a monk who was doing a rote task such as weeding a garden. The student asked the monk what he would do if he knew he only had a few minutes left to live. The monk replied, "I would keep weeding this garden." That's how I feel.

Purple
April 21st

You can't get purple without red.

I have a friend who once said that if she could get rid of anything in her life it would be the sexual abuse she endured from a favorite uncle as a young girl. She would keep the fire that destroyed her home and all of her possessions, her adopted daughter's drug addiction which led to her raising her drug-damaged grandchildren and many other trials. Just that one thing she couldn't accept.

She cried aloud about this to God one day, "Why this? Why did this one thing have to happen? I can take the rest."

She felt His Spirit ask her, "What is the character trait you are most proud of?"

She told me it is her ability to step into a crisis situation, know immediately what must be done and have the courage to swiftly take action. Even as she thought it, she saw the connection between that abuse and her developing this particular character trait. She *knew* she would not be that person without that incident. She loves this part of herself. And then she said, "I love purple. You can't get purple without red."

So often all we see of a person is the purple and not the red that got him there.

And we know that all things work together for good to them that love God, to them who are the called according to his purpose Romans 8:28

Sometimes You Have to Spell It Out
April 26th

For the last two weeks, I've been working on taxes and traveling on vacation, so I was praying for all the church problems to be held at bay (if the Lord wouldn't mind). Why would I ask such a thing? Why would He honor it? Someone has to do the work and that would be me. I was willing, but I needed to clear up a few things for Caesar first.

God must not have minded, because nothing happened for those two weeks. But the day after our return from vacation, everything happened with a vengeance.

Yesterday, five members of our congregation were in the hospital. I spent most of yesterday checking with people who were about to have surgery or just finished surgery, arranging for meals for when they return home and making sure family members are taken care of while they are in the hospital. People of all ages and with a variety of problems are in the hospital all on the same day.

Next time I pray for a bit of a break, I'll ask for the problems to be spread out a little after I get back.

No lists? How will I survive?
April 27th

During my quiet prayer time today, I had this thought, actually more of a command. *Give up your daily to-do list.* It's getting in the way of having constant communication with the Lord and being able to act on His direction immediately. I put things off, so that I can get through my list.

This came to me while I was thinking about Sister Kay. Her husband is seriously ill. I am walking with her today. That's what I do for her. I walk with her and we talk . . . or, she talks and I listen. Now and then I tell her a story from my life, then she does with it what she will. I was wondering how I could be there when needed, as often as needed, or when needed unexpectedly.

I was also thinking about how to have God's Spirit with me at all times, at every moment, when I had this thought. *Give up my daily to-do list.* A frightening thought. I've had a to-do list since I was 15 years old. I thought, *What if I forget something important?* I could almost hear God's chuckle. "Important to whom? If you give up the list and rely on Me, you'll accomplish what I think is important."

Does anything else matter?

Daily Life
May 3rd

Whew! Daily life takes so much time. The store, the mail catch-up, the laundry, the meals, the running around of the boys. That's all I've been doing for the last few days. It's 30 miles to the "big city" where we bank and the bigger stores where we stock up.

I survived the first week without a to-do list very well. I loved the relaxed let's-just-focus-on-this-one-thing-until-it's-done attitude that I ended up with. No list hanging over my head of other things I had to get to. Just left that up to the Lord. Once again, all that needed to be done was done. Anything not done, didn't matter.

I still made a short daily list to go over with the Lord. This is how all-knowing, all-seeing He is. Friday I had a huge block of time from about 10 A.M. to noon. I counseled with God as to what should go in there. He said not to worry about it.

My heart gave a tiny leap. Maybe a bit of time off? No. At 10 A.M. the school called. I had to go meet with the vice principal about one of our foster sons and a problem he was having. It took exactly until noon.

Selfish Server
May 4th

That's me. I'd like to be unselfish. I'd like to be like my sister Carol who loves to give and serve. When I point that out to her she says, "If I didn't want to do it, I wouldn't do it. I like doing it." That's the point! That's what makes her great. I am not. I don't want to do it. I know the Lord loves a cheerful giver, but even knowing that doesn't help. I'm a reluctant, whining giver.

Last night, I sat down for the first time in months with nothing to do. Nothing to do! Star Trek was on TV. I had just turned it on and realized it was an episode I had never seen! Not so unusual, given how seldom I watch TV. (We were a Nielsen Rating house for one month and had nothing to put in the diary. Sent back a "No Shows Watched" diary.) But tonight, it was just me and the Captain on the tube.

Then the telephone rang. Sister Kay needed a ride—a two-hour round trip for a medical emergency. I really wanted to say no and just watch Star Trek. Can you believe it? The very person I was praying about being sure I was available for when she needed help, and the Lord said to give up my to-do lists. So there it is. I have nothing to do. She needs help. But I just wanted to sit and watch Star Trek. After I went I was glad, but it was sure a fight with myself to say yes graciously.

Even worse, I started telling the Lord on the drive over that I couldn't do this too often given the price of gas. As if He can't handle that. As if He hasn't blessed me with more than I need. I realized how small I was being and apologized, but when I got home there was a new Internet order for one of our products with about 10 times the cost of the gas in profit. Just to make a point, I suppose.

How do people get to be like Carol? Is it even possible to change that much? Or will serving always be a struggle for me?

Manure
May 5th

Parker has been wanting manure for our 2,000-square-foot greenhouse. It takes a lot of manure to fill raised beds in a greenhouse that size. There's a place where he can get it a pickup-load at a time. It takes him four to five hours to drive over, fill up, come back and unload one truck load. He's been trying to talk the people who haul the manure from the Yosemite National Park pack animals to drop off one of their huge truck loads of manure but they say we live too far away

The last few weeks, he's been too busy serving others to get any manure. I can feel his frustration. Every day he says, "I'm going to go get another load of manure tomorrow" and every day, there's a new emergency. A single mom earning minimum wage with an old beater car needs a car repair to get to work, another person has a broken window, a friend needs help putting in electricity so he can move into his new trailer. Parker keeps saying he wishes he could get to the manure, and I keep nodding and asking if these people really need to be helped right now. But they do, and even if they didn't, Parker just can't say no to a person in need. Today he was out helping a mother just home from the hospital with a new infant. The pump on her well went out, and she has no budget to call the well man.

While he was gone, the Yosemite haulers called. They had one truckload of manure for us. One truck. Didn't sound like much. But every little bit. Then the truck showed up. This truck was the size of those double tractor trailers you see being hauled down the highway. It must have equaled 20 pickup loads dumped in our front yard. Parker was thrilled. Twenty pickup loads. Eighty hours of work! For free.

You know there aren't a lot of people that would see a mountain of manure dumped on their front lawns as a blessing. But that's the good thing about the Lord. The blessings are always custom tailored.

You just can't out give God.

Seeing People As God Sees Them: A Wisdom Prayer
May 7th

When I have a problem with people, I've learned to pray to see that person as God sees him or her.

The first time I prayed this prayer was when my son Daniel was a teenager. I thought he was arrogant. There is no other word for it. He started and lettered in three varsity sports, was in Advanced Placement classes, and had a lot of girls chasing after him. He was filled with pride and demands. We had reached the point where we could hardly have a civil conversation.

We lived in an area with a lot of families with only one or two children to support and both parents were working six-figure-income jobs. I made a good living, but there were 10 of us living on my one good income. Daniel was constantly on me for not spending enough time with them or giving them enough (cars, clothes, etc). His favorite line was, "You should have thought about how you were going to take care of us before you had us all." I'd say, "Daniel, even if I had the money for that, I wouldn't give it to you. Earn your own."

It reached the point where I couldn't think of one good thing to say about Daniel. I was praying about this when the thought came to me that I should pray to see Daniel as God saw him. So I did.

Shortly after that, I was at my mom's house leafing through one of her women's magazines. My eye was caught by an article about a boy who had reported a favorite teacher for molesting him. We'd had a similar incident in Daniel's middle school a year or two before, so I started reading it and realized the article was about our town and that incident.

It was presented from the boy's point of view. He'd been pilloried. The teacher was a favorite. There'd been petitions supporting the teacher, the local stores had signs up raising funds for his defense. The boy had been so mistreated by his peers at school that he had become seriously depressed and suicidal. He felt friendless and alone. He had only one sign of support. He had a note/petition framed and sitting on the table next to his bed. It was in support of him, but there were only four names on it. It was the only sign he'd had that anyone at all believed him, and it kept him going through the worst times. I knew Daniel's name was high on that list even though the article didn't mention the names. How did I know?

I remembered that day. I had dropped Daniel off at school and he had announced he was going to pass a petition around supporting the boy. Daniel was tired of the way the boy was being treated and thought someone should stand up for him. When I picked him up that afternoon, he was furious. The principal wouldn't let him do it. The principal wanted nothing more said or done about the incident in school. So Daniel and a few of his friends had signed it and given it to him.

I remember at the time agreeing with the principal. It was tearing the community apart. Just let it go. But now I saw it from the boy's eyes, a need Daniel had already seen and taken action on. I showed Daniel the article and apologized for my lack of support. After that, I noticed a lot of times Daniel was sensitive to others' needs and took action.

The second incident occurred around the same time. I attended a trade show in Dallas. It was a money-making show, but I don't work on Sunday, even if it means making less, a lot less—and the vendor knew it. Instead, I attended church, meditated, and spent the day in quiet contemplation. We were staying in a downtown hotel, so I attended an inner city church. When I walked in, it was clear these were very poor people.

And I, who have been in the same situation, was sitting there being incredibly judgmental. I couldn't believe myself. I'd look at an individual and think, *well, she might not be able to afford better clothes, but she doesn't have to wear mismatched plaids. Or, if he can't afford a barber, he could have a friend cut his hair. He sure needs it.* I was appalled by my own critical, snobbish attitude. I kept telling myself to shut up and feel the Spirit. Instead, I just kept right on, looking down on and judging people by how they looked.

It was so awful, I was ready to get up and leave for bringing such a bad spirit into the meeting. I finally prayed, God, I need help here. I'm going to have to leave if something isn't done about this. Please help me to see these people as you see them. The answer was immediate.

It was as if shackles fell off my eyes. The young man who

badly needed a haircut taught the adult Sunday school class. He started telling about his return to God—how he'd found a Bible laying in the trash and realized he'd done the same with God. And when he'd become religious, all his friends dropped him and how lonely he was before he'd found this church. I felt such awe for this young man who was willing to endure that loneliness for his love of God. All the people were nodding at him and smiling, the older lady in the mismatched plaids beaming such love at him, I felt I could touch it.

They became shining things to me. Tears were streaming down my face and the feelings of love and wonder were so strong, they were almost painful. I wanted to reach out and hug them and say, "Do you know how wonderful you are? How dearly God holds you?" I could hardly bear it. I remember thinking, *Isn't there an attitude in between judging them and seeing them as You see them? Because I don't think I can hold this much joy and sweetness. It's almost painful.*

This is one of those prayers God is quick to answer. I heartily recommend it.

Raising Boys
May 8th

A friend Mike came over a few nights ago and said abruptly, "Margaret, I sat up half the night thinking of a comment that would get a rise out of you, and you just blew it off. No reaction at all!" His wife Carol was sitting there, nodding her head in agreement. I have no idea what he'd just done to try to get this reaction. Then he went on, "I try and try and nothing gets to you."

I finally said, "After seven brothers and five sons, there isn't a lot you can come up with that they haven't already done and worse."

The following are just a few of the highlights:
○ I was checking out the fish tank one day years ago and real-

ized one was missing. I turned to my husband and said, "There's a fish missing. Isn't that odd?" And he said, "Oh no, He did eat it!" He was referring to the two-year-old who, I learned, had scooped up the fish and eaten it the day before.

○ Years later, the same boy came flying by me at top speed (well, top speed for a four-year-old) with a buddy right next to him, their eyes wide with fright. As they went past, they called to me, "We didn't start that fire!" I snagged a passing shirt, dragged it and the boy in it back and said, "Show me that fire you didn't start."

○ Another four-year-old once came in wailing, hands stretched out to the sides, with a molding strip nailed to his face. Yes, nailed to his face. Please don't ask how. I thought he was in bed when it happened.

○ Another night I poked my head into the dorm-style bedroom where all four of the children were sleeping (that's all we had at the time) and saw them kneeling beside their beds. The eldest was four years old, and the others were aged three, two and one. I turned on the light. They had finger-painted their sheets and were tacking the sheets to their mattresses. Ok, I can understand the finger paints, but why the tacks?

○ Matthias won the prize for youngest age for stitches out of all five of the boys—nine months old. Trying to walk down cement stairs.

○ Shortly after that incident, I went to work to support our family. The kids knew not to call me at work unless it was a true emergency, so I seldom received calls. Then one day, Elisabeth called and asked, "Did you tell Josiah he could jump out of the second story window using a black garbage bag as a parachute?"

I said (after a pause), "No, of course not." She then turned from the phone and yelled, "Josiah! Mom says quit jumping out of that window!" I was 20 miles away just raising my hands to God in prayer.

○ The same week Christian called. "I have a broken thumb."

"What makes you think you have a broken thumb?

Maybe it's just sprained."

"I'm sure it's broken. It looks exactly like my friend's thumb looked when he broke it doing the same break dancing move I was just doing."

Once again I sigh and shake my head. I now know the answer to the centuries-old question parents have been asking: "If your friend jumped off a cliff, would you jump off, too?" Yes, he would.

○ Matthias had just had his wisdom teeth pulled and he kept wanting me to look at the stitches. I said, "Matthias, I'm not looking at that." Parker did though. He went and got a flashlight and had quite the conversation with Matthias about it. I said to my older brother, "I can't believe it. He's 18 years old and I still have to look at his 'owies'." My brother said, "Be grateful he didn't ask you to kiss it better." (Yuck! He's the only one who can still get a rise out of me.)

○ Another brother, Jim, and I were talking a few weeks ago and he said, "I still have that voicemail you left me last Fall. My friends and I play it all the time and just laugh. It's great at parties." I said, "What voicemail is that? I never left you any funny voicemails." He said, "Well, it's mostly that you sound so calm. Most people would sound upset."

Here's what Jim heard on his voice mail:

Me: "Just one more thing Jim... Oh, wait. Here are the boys. What's that? (a pause and then garbled sounds). Is it alive or dead? (another pause and unintelligible sounds). Well. Gotta go, Jim. The boys brought me a rattlesnake in a bucket."

I'm not sure it's calmness. I think it's resignation.

The Church Grandmother
May 10th

We go to a small church. It's small enough that it feels like one big family, and the church grandmother is Sister Larue. She is 84. She watches and cares for everyone. If your son hasn't been coming out for a while and suddenly shows up and helps to pass the tokens of the Lord's supper, she notices and hugs him. If your son is dumb enough to walk down the chapel hall bouncing a basketball, she gives him a whack.

She notices when you are away and when you come back, she tells you how much she loves you, is glad you are back because she *really* missed you, and you know she means it.

She also broke open the candy-filled Christmas craft display last Christmas and ate part of it. A deed I'd been worried the teenagers would do. Well, of course, after they saw Sister Larue going for it, so did they. You have to watch her around sweets.

She's in a rehab center for physical therapy after an operation on her knee. She's been gone for a week and just wants to come home. I spoke with her yesterday and told her we would do all we could for her to get her home, but I hated to have her leave and suffer long-term damage. She's had no visitors. Why? Because she didn't tell anyone until Saturday where she was. We've been a little frantic looking for her again.

It's not the first time we've lost her. She "hates to be a bother." Now that we've found her, it's a problem that the rehab center is a three-hour, round trip drive. Most of the sisters work. We have a physical therapist in town, but he's not on her insurance list of providers. This is so frustrating!

I thought I had exactly four hours between the time I drop Matthias at school today and have to pick up Ryan for work. Then the boys informed me they get out of school early today. There will be fewer than four hours. My prayer this morning is to find a way to make it all work so I can get down to see her, cheer her up and still get back in time to get Ryan to work.

Trussed Up II
May 11th

I had to delete the original Trussed Up. The Spirit kept saying it wasn't true-which it wasn't. In that entry, I said that rather than walking hand in hand with the Savior, occasionally He had me trussed up-arm twisted up behind my back, hand clamped over my mouth, and the Spirit hissing in my ear. But the Spirit I feel is always kind, gentle and brings peace; I'm the one trussing myself up. It can be quite the struggle.

This is how the visit went with Sister Larue . . .

Wait . . . back up, back up. The day actually started with a walk with Sister Kay. As we walked she said, "I want to reach out to others. I don't know how to do it."

We walked in silence while I thought through the last year, and then I said, "It is hard for you. People just naturally come up and ask how things are. With you, for the last two years, things just keep getting worse. What can you say? 'Things are a lot worse' is sort of a conversation killer. I think it would help if you could quickly turn the conversation back to them. Know what's going on with them and bring that up. Or just take part in the small chitchat stuff. I think you need it. It'll take your mind off all the painful stuff going on at home and give you a break." She nodded her head the whole time. She said, "Last night when I sat next to you and just listened, it did help."

She had come over and sat next to me at our monthly women's meeting the night before. That's the meeting where we learn practical things and make those quilts we donate. A group of us were painting boards for a craft and just teasing and joking. Usually Sister Kay leaves before this part, but that night she stayed and just sat next to me and listened.

Today during this walk I noticed the roadside was covered with wildflowers. I picked a bunch for Sister Larue. I thought she might enjoy having a bouquet of mountain wildflowers in her room. Sister Kay gave me a card and a book to take to her with the wildflowers. She is always thoughtful.

After an hour and a half in a hot car with no air conditioning, I walked into Sister Larue's room with a slightly wilted (and bent) bunch of wildflowers in a vase. She said sternly, "I hope your name is on the bottom of that vase." I laughed one of those "Boy, was I wrong about how she'd react" laughs and said, "If it isn't, don't worry about getting it back to me. It's a dollar store vase."

We chatted for a while and then I went to see about getting her out of there. When her right knee was replaced, she was up and walking and home in four days. With the left it has been eight days and she is still not walking. I was told it would be painful for her to be driven to daily physical therapy, but she could leave if she wanted. I went back to her room and presented her options, "A few more days of boredom and unhappiness in the hospital or go home and risk never getting the full use of your knee back." I assured her I would support her in whatever she decided.

Then we sat in silence while she thought. Do you know a lot of people can't do that? After about 10 seconds of silence, they *have* to talk. I can handle it, so we sat in silence for about two minutes. Finally she said, "All right. I guess I'll stay for a few more days and then we'll see."

She started complaining about the food, not the hospital food. The food friends bring her. Last time she was ill, she told me "no food." But one sister took her a pasta salad anyway. She called to tell me it was good, how grateful she was, and she was sorry she had said no food. So I sent more sisters with food and took a meal myself. Sister Geneva took her chicken soup, which Sister Larue raved over at the time, "More of a stew than a soup-delicious."

Now she said, "But no food. Last time, Sister Ann brought pasta salad, and I hate pasta salad. And Sister Geneva brought that chicken soup, but she put all kinds of stuff in it. I just like plain chicken soup. I didn't like that at all." She made a face, then said, "And they always bring too much." Well, I knew who brought too much, so I said, "Ok, next time I'll only bring two pieces of chicken, not four." I nodded sympathetically, but now I was smiling at her-the smile I reserve for a crabby two year old.

"And," she said, "No visitors! I'm not bored, and I have nothing to talk about with anyone anyway."

I nodded yes, thinking, *Too bad. You're getting visitors. And by golly, I'm sending Sister Geneva over with food the minute you get home because she sits at home feeling depressed all the time. She needs to serve and you need to be served, so you can just eat what she brings and like it.*

But, of course, I didn't say this. Then as I left, after I had just told her I would call on Friday to find out how she was doing, she said, "And no calls. It's too hard to get to the telephone."

By now, I was smiling my "You know you're being unreasonable, but I love you anyway" smile and said in my brightest, cheeriest tone, "OK. I'll just call the head nurse and we'll talk about you behind your back. How about that?"

She laughed. After I got in my car, I started thinking that I would like to take a stick to some of these women. There's nothing in the handbook about **not** doing that, but I suspect it's one of those it-goes-without-saying things.

I know. I know. She was in pain and lonely and away from her own familiar house. She is not normally complaining or ungrateful. Still, I was thinking a good whack wouldn't hurt.

That night was the meeting I go to with Sister Kay. We've been going for eight months now and she has never said a word to anyone but me. Last night, she made a few small comments to a couple of other people. I was so touched by this. I knew what she was doing and what an effort it was for her. The others were oblivious. It was a normal thing to do, but not for Sister Kay.

Love songs
May 12th

A friend leaves love songs on my voicemail. This started 12 years ago when my oldest daughters were teenagers and my youngest daughter was 10 years old. At first, I thought it was for the teenagers, but after they grew up and moved away, the songs kept coming. They still keep coming. I think I've figured out who it is. It has slowed down. What used to come a couple of times a year is now every couple of years. I enjoy them.

I feel like I'm his Dulcinea... if a grandmother can be a Dulcinea.

A Love Song from God
May 12th

God sent me a love song once, too. Here's how it happened.

You might think that when I accepted the calling of Relief Society president and started spending all my time serving others, that I would immediately be blessed. But that isn't how God works. It's after the show of faith that the blessings come.

I wasn't surprised when, shortly after I was called to serve, I was in a major car accident. To accept the call, I had to stop traveling as a computer consultant. I put aside enough money to cover four months of expenses. I expected to spend that four months building up our Internet business to the point it would cover expenses.

After the car accident, I couldn't sit at a computer at all without tears flowing from the pain. It was six weeks before I could spend more than 15 minutes on the computer at a time. Now, I was generating no income and quickly going through all the money I had set aside, especially with the additional medical bills.

But I kept serving and praying daily for my tasks. They seldom had anything to do with generating money. The money dribbled in little by little; usually just in time to cover final notices.

I was sitting at my desk late one afternoon in November, after five months of this, and said, "You know, God, I am going to keep serving just as I have been. I trust You and I appreciate the money that has come, but it is a little discouraging to always be paying final notices and only one at a time. I'm wondering if You've forgotten that it takes money to live here on earth. But, if that's the way You want it, I can accept that. If I lose it all, I lose it all. I'll keep serving." I meant it. And God knew I meant it. Just then the phone rang.

A client was in a big hurry to place a large order—$11,000 in profit. Would I immediately fax a proposal? Would I mind if they FedExed a check so I could ship the next day? (Oh no, please don't do that!) *They* kept thanking *me*!

I couldn't believe it. I'd have been happy with a thousand dollars.

I paid off enough debt that my expenses dropped to the amount the Internet was bringing in at the time, and we still had money for our Christmas trip back East to see my children.

Now, it's a few months later. I am thinking about Gwen, the woman who put together the Weigh Down® program. She said God sent her love songs and she shared a few experiences. I was feeling kind of lonely, and I asked God if He would mind showing me a little extra love that day. I was afraid He'd think I wanted more money, so I said, "I don't need money. I just need to know You love me. Gwen gets songs. I think I'd like one, but if You even just want to send me a butterfly or something, I'd be happy."

Then I took off in my car to do my good deed for the day—helping a sister organize her pantry, which, to be frank, was a big mess, but she's not an organizer, and I am. I was listening to the end of an audio tape on the way and when it finished, I popped it out. A song was playing on Ryan's favorite country western station. As I reached to turn it off I felt the Spirit whisper, "Here's your song." It was just the chorus from the song "26 Cents" by the Wilkinsons. They sing about a mother telling her daughter she can call anytime, anytime at all. Her mother knows she needs more than money, she needs her mother's love.

But in my mind I heard Father in place of mother. Now isn't that just perfect? I love the part about needing more than money.

Other People's Prayers
May 14th

Matthias is weed whacking, cleaning up fallen branches, building burn piles, and clearing away brush as his "job"— a big moneymaker this time of year in fire country. Saturday, he was doing four burn piles as the final cleanup for Sister Sue, the first counselor in the Relief Society presidency. When I dropped him off, I started worrying one might get out of control, causing massive damage or hurting Matthias.

I said a quick prayer and immediately was reassured.

I picked him up later. He told me a freak gust of wind had come up and shot sparks outside his cleared line, causing one of the piles to go out of control. Flames were arcing up toward the overhanging oily leaves of the white oaks when he looked up and saw Sister Sue standing on the porch holding her cell phone. He called up to her to bring a bucket, which she did promptly. Since she had her phone in her hand, she also called 911 immediately. He said, "The fire department came, but I already had it out. I spent 20 minutes running back and forth to the pond, beating on flames and pouring water before it was out."

The firemen were great. They said his burn pile was

done within guidelines, and it was just one of those freak things. They suggested he get an application and apply to be a firefighter since he's old enough (18) and did such a good job. Matthias said not a chance; he was exhausted from the effort and the worry. The firemen soaked the ground to be sure the fire stayed out and left.

Here's the background for Matthias's protecting Hand.

Sunday, Sister Sue was giving the lesson on the Holy Ghost, and she told her version of the burn pile fire. She told the class that I've been encouraging her for months to go to the Lord to get her errand for the day, so she decided to give it a try on Saturday. She wanted to work on her Sunday lesson, but no, she was to get her Mother's Day meal prepared. She did that and said, "Ok, now my lesson?" But, no, she should make phone calls. She said, "I made three calls, but no one was home. I was thinking 'Is this a joke?' when I walked out on the deck and looked over to see one of the burn piles out of control. Matthias called up for a bucket which was right in front of me. I ran it down to him, and then realized I had my phone in my hand, so I called 911 right away. If I hadn't been making the calls, I wouldn't have had the phone."

On the way home from church, I told Matthias why Sister Sue happened to have the phone in her hand and walk out onto the deck at just the right moment.

A lot of times, people are oblivious to how often they are blessed and protected because of the prayers and righteous living of the people surrounding them.

It's About Focus
May 15th

I was thinking today about focus. I realize my diary must read oddly to people who don't believe in God, but I don't know how to talk or write about my life without bringing Him into it. When I was 20 years old, a professor once asked how we made decisions. My answer was, "First, I check with God to see if He has an opinion." At times He does, other times He doesn't. For some people, it doesn't matter whether you become a hairdresser or a librarian. For others, it's very important to Him.

I've learned a lot by keeping my attention on God. I've learned to be grateful for all things, even the things that look bad at first. I've learned that after the trial of my faith come the blessings. I've learned that all things work for good for those who love God, so no one can ever really hurt me. God can turn anything to my advantage. I've learned that forgiveness fills me with peace. Not infrequently, all I can do is want to want to forgive and God will do the rest. (Yep, I really meant for both of those want to's to be in there.) Because I'm willful and rebellious, these lessons have been hard and painful to learn.

How I react depends on my focus. I think of Paul being beaten, stripped and thrown into prison. He sings praises to God at midnight. I realize it's because his focus was on bringing people to God, that he knew God could use this situation to convert many. And he praised God for it. If his focus had been on building wealth and living a comfortable life, he would have been angry and bitter at being beaten and thrown in to prison.

When I've gotten lost unexpectedly or run into delays, I've learned to look around me to see if God wants me there to help an individual. Often, that's exactly why I'm there.

Once my husband and I were lost in a bad part of a city late at night. We were concerned for just ourselves when we saw a car on the side of the road with small children milling around outside of it. My husband pulled over. We found a young mother with a car that wouldn't start. We gave her battery a jump and sent her on her way. Then we quickly found our original destination with no more problems. See? The Lord put us where we were needed. If I'm living righteously, I need to just look around for those who need me when I end up in situations like that.

If I just stay focused on God life is a series of blessings, not obstacles.

Life is Like a Video Game
May 17th

"Why," Matthias asked again, "do the good seem to suffer the most?" Here's my new analogy.

Because life is like a video game, and they're on Level 50. You, down here at Level 2 can't understand how they can deal with a level 50 problem. Suppose we really are on earth to learn and to grow. Of course, Level 50 obstacles and trials are harder. So are Level 50 skills and strengths. Level 2 is a snap to a Level 50 player. How could a Level 50 player keep growing without Level 50 obstacles?

"Oh," people say. "I don't want to be good if it means I'll suffer more." I don't know. Maybe it's relative. Level 2 obstacles can be just as painful to a Level 2 player as Level 50 obstacles are to a Level 50 player. I don't mean to trivialize this. Unlike a video game, in life, the pain is real. But, so is the joy.

For Matthias—who once again made Family Home Evening a less-than-joyful experience as he questioned God.

Robin
May 23rd

I prayed once to have a friend, and God sent me Robin. We met each other through church service (the Visiting Teaching program – we visit assigned sisters to ensure all is well or if needed to offer help and comfort) and slowly became best friends. One day, I realized she was the friend God sent me in answer to that prayer.

One of the great things about Robin is that she loves to

shop. I hate it, so whenever I had to go, I'd call Robin. Anytime, night or day, she was up for shopping. The best thing about clothes shopping with Robin is that she uses it as a chance to give compliments. These are actual "Robin quotes." She'd say, "Oh not that. That's too boring. You need clothes as vibrant and fun as you are." Or "That's perfect. It makes your incredible blue eyes sparkle." (Wow! Who wouldn't want to shop with Robin?)

She uses the word *love* easily and gives hugs freely. I needed that, since for the last five years of my first marriage, my soon-to-be ex-husband lived in a different room. It would have been easy to start a relationship with another man at that point. They were so available and so free with their compliments. When I realized how tempted I was, I went to the Lord and said, "I need a friend I can count on to point out what's good about me and to give me hugs." And here came Robin.

She was with me throughout the divorce, the moving and the struggles with the children after the divorce. We walked around the lake we both lived on almost daily, and then sat and talked on the bench behind my house.

Two-and-a-half years after the separation and divorce, I decided I was ready to start dating again. My first "date" was with a man who was not a believer in God, Christianity or keeping chaste before marriage. It was set for Monday, President's Day. While I was sitting in church the day before my big date, I felt the Spirit tell me I shouldn't be dating non-believers and when I got home, I would have a message on my voicemail canceling. Sure enough, there was the message on voicemail when I got home. Big family emergency, and he had to go out of town and cancel.

That afternoon, I made a date with another non-believers friend who had heard I was finally dating. Again I made it for Monday President's Day. Monday morning I spent time communing with God. I got the same message. I shouldn't be doing this. Once again, I said, "So I'm just supposed to call and cancel?" And the Spirit said, "It's taken care of."

One final message. Do it again, and you will be allowed to suffer the consequences of your poor judgment. "For my spirit will not always strive with man," says the Lord in Genesis 6:3. The Lord wouldn't be stepping in again. Well, hey, I know a reprimand and a warning when I hear one. I decided I wouldn't make any more dates with men who weren't keeping high Christian standards, but I was not happy about it.

I got home and sure enough, I got a call. The transmission had just gone out on my friend's car. He had to take care of that and cancel on the date.

I called Robin all whiny and crying. I went to her house where she brushed my hair while I complained. See? She's like my best friend from third grade, playing with hair styles and makeup. I told her I'm just tired of working all the time and being responsible for my kids, my employees and my clients. I want to go out and have someone take care of me for a while and just laugh and have fun. Is this so terrible?

Robin said, "I don't know, Margaret. I just know God loves us and wants to bless us." My perfect friend sent to me from God. She didn't agree with my complaints, but she did sympathize and testified to me of eternal truths.

I took my complaints to the Lord and was told that within six months, I would meet the man I was to marry. I thought, "For Pete's sake, all I want is a date or two, not some marriage thing." It wasn't a promise I was happy about. I told my aunt Donna that I knew God was trying to give me a gift, but I didn't want the gift. She said, "You haven't even met the gift. How do you know whether or not you want the gift?"

Robin moved just before I met Parker. I was so lonely without her, I was open to him. If she'd still been around, I doubt I would have paid any attention to Parker.

Robin is still my best woman friend. When I had to make a decision between Parker and another man, a large part of why I chose Parker is because, in the best ways—service, listening, caring—he reminded me of Robin, my friend sent by God.

A Day in the Life of . . .
May 26th

Wake

Chat with Parker. Tell him my decision about decorating the house. He keeps telling me I can't hang things on the walls or have certain things in the house. Decide that he acts as if I have to have permission to decorate, because I let him. Decide to tell him that I clean the house, do the laundry and fix the meals. In return for doing the wife things, I get the wife perks. Meaning, I get to decorate the house according to my personality. And I am going to. He should trust that if he likes me, he'll like the result and that my motives are good. I want to create a warm and welcoming environment for family and friends. Even if I do not like the country look. He says nothing, gets up, dresses and heads to the city to take care of required building licenses. I hang things on the wall while he's gone.

Read scriptures. One jumps out at me. Phillipians 2: 14 says, "Do all things without murmurings or disputings." Dwell on this for a while. Was I disputing this AM? Mmm . . . maybe, maybe not. Depends on whose point of view you're looking at it from—mine or Parker's.

Pray

Write in journal

Read emails. Answer Bible question for person who visited our web site and emailed us. Easy one. "What do BC, BCE and AD stand for?"

Read and like ONE forward from Aunt who sends about ten a day.

Read Washington Post on-line. Note media is becoming even more hostile in attitude toward Israel. See Armageddon dynamics in place.

Read Miss Manners. People still acting like people.

Talk with daughter Flora.

Shower and do my fifteen minute exercise routine 50 sit-ups, 12 pushups, 20 lunges and a few stretches.

Reward myself with 10 minutes of reading. Two chapters of a Robert B. Parker Spenser mystery. I read fast.

Go down to barn and gather ingredients and jars for pickling eggs. Have never done this. Have never eaten a pickled egg. Brother Mike (the man who can't get me to react no matter what he tries) has assured me that pickled eggs are good and we do have four dozen in the fridge and more coming every day. I get the recipe from his wife. I figure if we don't like them, we can always give them to him, so I'd better use his recipe.

Put dishes away from drainer from last night. Peel half the eggs.

Ryan comes in. Time for him to go to school. It's 8:20. Until today, he was attending early morning scripture study and had to be at the church at 7:00 every school morning—our method of keeping kids chaste. Scripture study every morning for one hour before school during the four years of high school. If the scriptures don't do it, maybe keeping them exhausted will.

Run Ryan to school. 15 miles round trip. Stop at store on way back for egg-pickling supplies.

Get home and pickle the eggs. Turns out a dozen fit in a quart jar. We have mostly Banty eggs, so some are small. Could fit one more, but decide I am superstitious enough that I don't want to risk botulism because of the 13th egg. Take it back out and eat it for breakfast.

Get a call from a sister in the church who has just been diagnosed as having a chronic illness. Wants to be released from being a Visiting Teacher. Tells me the husband of one of the sisters she visits has just lost his job, so if we know of any available, to call her. She says she'll do visiting teaching one more month. She says she needs to concentrate on herself.

Visiting teaching takes about four hours a month. Unless, of course, most people decide they can't do it. Then the burden falls on the few who do, and it will take more than four hours per month. In other words, it's not a huge sacrifice. It is an opportunity to serve God by serving His children, since that's what visiting teaching is about. But this is between this sister and God. The calling isn't from me. I tell her I'm re-doing the routes, so I'll keep her request in mind. I'm always re-doing the routes. I tell God I could use a little more compassion. I don't see chronic illness as an excuse for not doing visiting teaching. Parker has a chronic illness and he manages to keep serving. Time to pray again to see people as He sees them.

Talk with Matthias while I am finishing the eggs. He starts work at a local restaurant tonight. We discuss his work apron, pickled eggs, people who use the butter knife for peanut butter and then put it back on the butter plate (that would be Parker), the HSFestival (rock concert) in DC, which we will miss this year, and the 4th of July (he'd rather be on the Smithsonian Mall in DC, not here).

Wash up the few dishes from breakfast and pickling eggs. It is now 9:30 AM—time to get a move on if I want to get anything done today.

Call Brother John and tell him about sister whose husband lost job. Call two people I know were looking for workers to see if they still are. Call the sister whose husband is out of work, but her line is busy. Put that on hold for a while.

Take call from Josiah who wants Daniel's number. We discuss his father-in-law who just found out he has lung cancer that has already spread to his brain. Not good news. Hope to see him while I'm back there for son Christian's wedding.

Decide this is a dumb idea for an entry. Will write a few more words and end it. Rest of the day is more of the same. Plan to meet with Tom, a local massage therapist and instructor, to go over his web site, visit-teach two sisters before and after the post office run, pick the boys up from school, make dinner, talk with Parker, and get the material out to make a dress tomorrow to wear to the rehearsal dinner for Christian' wedding. Work on our web site in between. An hour a day, whether I want to or not.

At night I sit and watch videos while I work on afghans-that would be hand-crocheted blankets, not the dogs. Watched *Gal-*

axy Quest last night and laughed out loud all the way through it. Guess you just have to have been addicted to the original series and then read a bunch of books on the behind-the-scenes shenanigans. Parker just stares at me. But Matthias also loves it. Matthias and I clap like the aliens at the end, and Parker rolls his eyes. Finish one more strip on one of the afghans. **Say prayer and fall into bed.** Still haven't re-done those visiting teaching routes.

Why Didn't You?
June 6th

I just read three articles and listened to a niece who all asked the same questions. "How could God let this happen? Why didn't He stop the Holocaust? Why doesn't He stop people from hurting small children? What kind of God would allow these things to happen?"

I believe we knew the deal before we came here. This is a practice life with a practice body. We get our eternal bodies later. We came down here with our agency. God will not take it from us. So, just as He won't stop us from hurting other people, from saying or doing mean and hateful things, from running up our credit cards, stuffing our faces with food, being unfaithful to our spouses, neither will He stop others. That is our job. That is our job!

It's as if we haven't figured out we're down here together, and the world is what we make it. As if we haven't learned from Jesus Christ, Gandhi and Martin Luther King—and numerous others who persist in nonviolent methods of change— that it is possible for us to change the world we live in by using love, strength and courage.

When I hear of a child being kidnapped, I do not ask why God doesn't do something. I ask why we, as a people, do not immediately bring the entire country to a standstill until that child is found. No gas, food, entertainment— nothing until that child is found. All of us out beating the streets and bushes; how often would incidents like this continue to happen if we as a people responded this way?

I hear people say, "When I get up there I'm going to insist God explain why He didn't stop these things from happening." You know what I think He'll say?

"Why didn't you?"

Forgiveness
June 8th

Not a lot is going on here today, so I thought I'd tell my forgiveness story. You know how there is a particular defining moment where you finally get a concept? This story is that moment for me.

I had been pressured by the Spirit to go through my life and forgive every grudge I still held. The small things, such as the time I was walking with five children under the age of six. Three in a buggy, two holding on to each side, when one let go in the middle of crossing a busy street. A woman in a passing car leaned out of her car and screamed at me to take care of my little girl. That was a big help! Did she see me with any extra hands? I needed to forgive her.

I also needed to forgive the bigger things. The things I'd rather not talk about. I kept putting it off because it occurred to me that the next step might be asking others to forgive me. Whoo. Not up for that. Humbling myself is not my favorite approach to life.

Anyway, I had started a forgiveness journal, and every time I remembered an incident that still bothered me, I forgave. Or if I couldn't forgive, I prayed to the Lord telling Him I wanted to forgive and asking for His help. This is when I learned the Lord would help even if the best I could pray was "I want to want to forgive." (Once again both of those "want to's" are in there on purpose)

I learned more than that. I learned that there are people I didn't want to forgive because I was afraid if I forgot about it, so would He and then this person who deserved punishment wouldn't get it. I learned to give up my vindictive spirit.

I learned true peace comes from forgiving. There was a big drop in the number of misunderstandings and upsetting experiences as I learned to apply forgiveness quickly. I learned driving in rush hour traffic is an excellent place to practice forgiveness on demand.

Then this awful thing happened. I had just started my own business and was having a tough time financially. Christmas was coming and I still had six children at home. I was bidding on a consulting/software contract. A friend wanted the software and training. He knew I knew the product, so he asked me to get the software for him. But, unfortunately for me, it was a government agency, and it had to go out to bid.

I contacted one of the resellers for the software and told him I only wanted the consulting side, but it was a joint proposal. Would he bid this together with me and he'd get the software sale? He told me he was happy to do it since he had no consultant who could train on it. We discussed pricing. Then, behind my back he submitted a separate bid, underbid me which was easy to do, since he knew my pricing and took the whole deal.

We had a short and angry conversation about his underhanded way of dealing with me. I was jogging in the mornings at the time, and every morning for three weeks I came home more upset than when I left because I kept thinking about this. Finally, I said to God, "I'll do whatever it takes, but I have to stop thinking about this. It's ruining my life. I think I've forgiven him and then I start thinking about it again."

God said, "Call him."

I thought what a dumb idea. "I'm supposed to call a man I've never personally met, who hasn't asked for forgiveness, and say what? 'I forgive you for being such an underhanded slimeball?' Naaah. I'll just handle this my own way. I'm not doing that. I can forgive without calling him. I forgave that lady who screamed at me instead of offering to help me with my children crossing the road."

Another week goes by and I'm still upset, so I say, "OK, I'll do it. Whatever it takes."

"But," I say to God, "I don't know what to say when I call. What shall I say?"

God says, "Ask him to forgive you."

I say in my mind, *are you crazy? He is the evil deed doer, not me! Forget it. I'm not doing that.*

Another couple of days and I really can't stand this unhappiness, so I say, "OK. You win. Ask him to forgive me for what?"

God says, "Ask him to forgive you for thinking he's such an underhanded slimeball." Right. Even if he *is* an underhanded slimeball, I'm not supposed to think he's an underhanded slimeball? But this time, I am ready to do what it takes.

I call his office and we play telephone tag for a while, so I use the secretary as the go-between and ask her to let him know it's important that we speak and I'm not upset, but I do need to speak with him. He tells her to have me call him at his home that night, which I do.

When I get him on the line, I say in New Jersey mode (meaning very fast), "I'm calling to ask you to forgive me for thinking you're such an underhanded slimeball."

He says, "What?" I repeat it, slower. And he says again, "What?"

I repeat it again, much slower. "I'm calling to ask you to forgive me for thinking you're such an underhanded slimeball."

He says, "Oh, that's OK. A lot of people think that." I roll my eyes up to God and think . . . *see?*

But you know what? I no longer care. I am completely at peace. It's such an incredible feeling for me. After weeks, literally weeks, of being upset by this, of having my early morning run ruined every day by thinking about this, I am finally at peace about it. And now when I think about it, it is with joy that such a miracle could happen. I almost weep in relief.

Now I *want* to go around asking people to forgive me for any mean or cruel things I have done so that they can feel the same thing. I think perhaps they are having a hard time forgiving because I haven't apologized and if apologizing will help, I'm going to do it. I want everyone to feel this way.

Two more things. I almost hate telling this part because it's so American to think it's about the money when it isn't. But he asks me if I'll do the consulting part since he really doesn't have anyone who can. I say yes to that, which means I end up getting what I wanted in the first place—the consulting part of the job.

Then he asks me to meet with him to discuss joint marketing this software. So I turn to God and say, "If I truly forgive him, does that mean I have to work with him? He still doesn't think what he did was wrong. He never did apologize or ask me for forgiveness."

God says, "You need to forgive and forget, but you don't have to be stupid about it."

I take that to mean that working with a liar is a dumb idea since I sell on integrity and keeping my word, so I don't partner with him. But it's OK. I did forgive him completely, and that's what mattered. He never changed. It didn't affect him at all, only me.

I love forgiveness. I love the feeling of peace and contentment it brings.

Parker's Magic Barn
June18th

You can find anything and everything in Parker's barn. People call here two or three times a week to ask Parker if he has X,Y or Z in his barn. He usually does. Here are some of the things Parker has had in his barn.

A $100 replacement part for a metal detector that he picked up at a garage sale for $10 and then used it to swap the local mechanic for a part for my car

A pink toilet for a bathroom

A stove

A refrigerator

Four metal-framed windows

A lovely, hexagonal aquarium on a wooden base

Darkroom equipment

An organ

I told Parker I wanted a tall, wood-paned window for our entryway, and he said he had one in the barn. He did, too. It even has a screen, and the window swings open using a hand crank on the inside to let in summer breezes.

When my sister came to visit, she said it was too bad we didn't have a rowboat for our pond. Parker said he had one in the barn. I said, "Parker, there is no way I missed seeing a *rowboat* in the barn." But apparently, I had missed the 10-foot rowboat stored along with everything else in there.

See? It is magic.

Still Alive
June 21st

I did feel I was going to die this year. I discussed it with Parker and with a couple of close friends. One friend asked if it could be God wanted me to reconsider my life.

That was a possibility. I remember one blunt conversation with God. I was considering taking a job rather than doing consulting. It was a great job – on paper. A base of $260,000 plus bonuses, world travel and the chance to wear good suits and get expensive haircuts again. The consulting business I was doing brought in a lot less than that.

I convinced myself that since Parker liked to travel and Matthias was about to head off to college that this was a great opportunity. I could take the job and Parker, who is retired, could come along for many of the trips. Win, win right?

God told me bluntly that He hadn't put me together with Parker so I could take off traveling the world chasing after money. We had all we needed and much of what we wanted. God had things for us to accomplish. That meant *us* not just me with Parker along for the ride. If I wasn't going to do what needed to be done here He would just take me home to Him. God would send Parker another helpmeet who would actually be a helpmeet. Um that's clear enough.

That message was part of the driving force behind this year of praying daily for my task from God. That and a need to figure out what I was supposed to be doing – or what Parker and I were supposed to be doing. We pray together daily in addition to our individual private prayers. Daily actions and choices create daily habits create character and create a life. I am getting not just a new life but becoming, slowly, a new person.

I am no longer a computer consultant but am Internet marketing a product that Parker had been selling through magazine ads. I am spending more and more time searching out and caring for those in need. I do some of that alone. But often, because Parker is also in the leadership of our church, we go together or counsel together about how to take care of those needs.

I still worried that I might die, even at one point asking for a blessing without telling the elder giving me the blessing why I wanted it. I was assured in that blessing that I had much left to accomplish here on earth.

Spring is now officially over. I didn't die and I no longer believe I will any time soon.

Times I Didn't Die
June 22nd

I occasionally pull out the times I didn't die and peer at them with my mind, with my heart slightly anxious as I relive those moments.

○ The time I was on a tractor full of kids in Nova Scotia and I fell off. My head was on the ground just inches from the slowly, but inexorably moving, large back tire. There was not enough time to even think about it, much less to move—just the awareness of my head and that tire. Then the tire suddenly bounced up and over my head, clearing my face by mere inches and landing just inches on the other side of my head. "Must have been a rock," we all decided as we quietly stood, the laughing stopped, trying to figure out how I'd narrowly escaped death by tractor.

○ I was on that same tractor a year or so later, heading as fast as I could across our fields. I wasn't working, just driving that tractor for the fun of it. I hit a deep furrow and the tractor turned almost sideways, then suddenly righted itself. I turned it off and sat and pondered my once again near escape. I did drive much more slowly across the fields after that.

○ There was the time I was in the middle of a New Jersey freeway with my two young brothers in the back seat. Traffic was moving swiftly when I screeched to a halt. The car in front of me had stalled on the freeway. Traffic behind me was just barely able to part and go to either side of us like a stream forking at a bank. I waited and waited for a break so that I could also pull off to one side and continue on my way. Finally, putting on my hazards, I thought, *I'll just get out and tell the driver that when traffic eases up that I'll push him off to the side, since we seem to be stuck here together.* I had barely stepped out of my car when a car behind us didn't make the lane change and smashed into the back of my car. My brothers were safe in a little opening on the passenger side. The engine occupied the space where my body had been a second before and the steering wheel had been pushed through the seat into the back seat area, and the trunk was folded up into the back seat. The tow truck driver later said of the accident, "No one made it alive out of that car." But we did.

○ The same freeway later. A different car. Rain was pouring down in one of those New Jersey onslaughts, and we were approaching a sharp curve, but no one slowed down. Going 65 mph on a rain-slick highway into a sharp curve surrounded by cars brought the thought to me, ***What would you do if a tire blew out just now? Not a slow leak, but a loud, explosive tire blowout.*** I was holding fast to the steering wheel thinking about how I would handle it, thinking ease up on the gas, but don't hit the brakes when—just as I entered the curve—the tire did blow out. I was holding tight and managed to control the car so there was no spinning out of control. I eased up on the gas and didn't hit the brakes. As I stopped on the side of the freeway, people came to help saying, "I don't see how you managed to control that car. Good job."

There are more, but I have to leave. We're going to a church meeting today. I'm happy to still be here.

Empty Nest
June 23rd

Matthias leaves Friday. After 30 years of raising children, I am finished. I am sad. I said to Parker, "Matthias leaves Friday. This time, he won't be coming back, and I'm sad." Parker said, "Are the boys in the office?" That didn't comfort me.

He then went on to tell me some things about the car, to tell me about arrangements he'd made for a meeting tomorrow, and then he fell asleep. I lay there thinking, *I don't care about the car. My last child is leaving home.*

Are all men this lacking in empathy, or is it just Parker? Excuse me, but I think I'm angry. No. I know I'm angry. I'm sad and hurting. Parker is hoping this will go away and is avoiding the conversation. Does he not realize that attitude puts him right in the line of fire? I think I'll just write instead.

I remember 30 years ago when I was expecting my first child, who turned out to be Michael. I remember going into the bedroom and opening the drawer where I'd stored all the little clothes I'd made and just taking them out and smelling them. Thinking about what it would be like to have a child of my own. Not knowing it would open up places in my heart that had never existed before. Not even thinking of this day coming.

How do I close those doors, those rooms in my heart? What can possibly fill them? Before I was looking forward, and now I'm looking back. Before I was being stretched to the limit, and now I'm being diminished.

It makes sense to me now that women shrink as they age. All the milk in the world can't fill this gap. Milk—that warm, flowing fluid from our breasts with which we once nourished and comforted our infants. Ironic that once we no longer have a need to produce it, that we need it ourselves to keep from diminishing. Is this coming full circle? Can I make something of that?

I could come up with a list of platitudes to calm and cheer myself. I choose to grieve instead.

I re-read this and think to myself, *Oh, quit being a drama queen. You've been grieving in advance for months, and it's getting a little old. Go give Parker a hug and get to sleep. I think I'll take my own advice and do just that.*

Final Cleaning
June 24th

Cleaning up the few things Matthias left in his room after dropping him at the train station in Sacramento. He will be in Denver tomorrow night.

Found the following:
5 glasses
2 bowls
3 plates
6 pieces of silverware
A 10K gold ring with a cubic zirconium (?)
4 pieces of paper with girls' telephone numbers and reminders to call before he left (He didn't.)

What he did on his last day home:
Went to school.

Left school and washed his whites at the Laundromat. Came back to school and made up one test so he could actually pass his Advanced Biology class and graduate.

Stood in a corner for five minutes in Advanced Biology for talking too much and making a balloon make squeaky noises. "The balloon was talking, too, asking why we couldn't just go home," is his explanation. I tell Matthias that action is a good argument for bringing back corporal punishment. He says he made his teacher laugh every day, and if he hadn't been in her class, she would have led a dull, boring life with no happiness or laughter in it. I snort.

Went swimming at the Octogon—a natural pool surrounded by sixty-two-foot cliffs for jumping off. Matthias lives to tell the tale of the old guy (who looked to be about 38) who did a pike off the cliff.

Bought new $72.00 sunglasses with his graduation money. Me: "You'll lose those in a week. Why not get something that will last?"

Matthias: "I need these for my new job as a groundskeeper at the apartments. Do you want me to go blind from sun stroke?"

I suggest a $10 pair would do just as well. "Not for attracting girls," says Matthias.

Finally Matthias's reign as the student with the most detentions for being late to class and talking too much is over. I actually got a call from the principal one day to point that out to me. I said, "Are you inviting me to the awards ceremony?" What else could I say? I worked on that for 12 years. Matthias just never understood why teachers were always interrupting his social life with boring academic stuff.

Matthias and His New Home
June 26th

I called Daniel's house to talk with Matthias, because I do miss him. Daniel's wife Jen answered. She said, "It sure must be quiet there with Matthias gone."

I said, "Oh, have you noticed it's a little noisier with Matthias around?"

She said, "Yep. He's kind of loud. And busy. Daniel's much quieter."

I laughed. Matthias is, and always has been, a noisy, active, energetic kid. I called him Electric Man when he was little. When he was three years old and Daniel was five, Daniel came in and asked his dad if he couldn't keep Matthias in with him for a while because Matthias was "giving him a headache."

Hope this month together works out.

Life of Ease
June 27th

That's what I'm living right now with Matthias gone and Ryan out of school. I have three extra hours every day since I am no longer the designated driver. I can take on a long project without having to stop and run a boy to town.

Yesterday, a friend and I tracked down T-shirts for making T-shirt dresses. Cut a few inches off the bottom of a T-shirt, sew a gathered piece of coordinated material to it and . . . voila! A little girl's dress. The church Humanitarian Aid center said that was their greatest need right now. They said *no more* quilts, please. They are overstocked.

We are making quilts in our group to give to Child Protective Services for local children who are taken from their homes. In the process, I learned color does have an affect on our emotions. After spending a few hours sewing together a quilt top of yellow material scraps, I was practically giddy with happiness.

Now I have T-shirts laid out on our bed, with matching material scraps on top. Parker was kind enough to come in and make nice comments about them—after a little prodding from me. Seeing them reminded him he needed a few rips and tears sewed up, so I did that this morning. See what making nice comments gets you? Mended clothes.

And I'm finally unpacking the last of the boxes we moved into the barn when I married Parker three years ago. The house is finished enough that I can do it. Also, we were given a china cabinet for free. I have actually been praying about it.

Oh, I know there are people who think you shouldn't, but I pray about everything. I wasn't sure what would go well with my rather unique dining room set. I've never seen another like it, and the company that made it is out of business. Then this perfect cabinet showed up in Parker's Magic Barn. After calling two other families that I knew might want it and being told they didn't, I get to keep it and unpack my good dishes.

Well, after we do a little staining and varnishing. It's already sanded down.

Now I'm worrying about unpacking my dishes. What if there's an earthquake? Parker just rolls his eyes. He insists there are no earthquakes here, but there was a small one on a weekend we were out of town.

I'm doing all this work today in total solitude and enjoying it. I miss Matthias most at the dinner table and when we're having family prayer. But in the middle of the day, I enjoy the quiet.

CTR Rings in the Trash
June 29th

I wear a silver ring with the letters CTR on it. The letters stand for Choose The Right. When I was really angry with God, I would rip off my silver CTR ring and toss it in the trash. It wasn't, as the saying goes, that life is one thing after another. It's that it's the same darn thing over and over. I forget who first said that.

About seven or eight years ago, one of those things that seems to happen over and over, happened again. I went through my rant of, "What's the point of church? Nothing changes. God is no help," and off went the ring into the trash. (Oh. Maybe that's where Matthias gets it from.) As I threw it, I realized I wasn't as angry as usual, and that I had a choice in how I felt.

I stood there wondering what to do. I was just overwhelmed and tired of the fight with life. I kept thinking to call Sister Rochelle. Sister Rochelle has also dealt with the same problem over and over. Three of her children died of different diseases as children or in their teens. Now a fourth had an incurable disease and was sinking quickly. He was 30 years old at the time and the father of five small children. I thought, if anyone can understand these feelings, it would be Sister Rochelle.

She has certainly had to deal with the same thing over and over, and there's no way it could be said it's her own fault.

I called, and here's how the conversation went.

I said, "Sister Rochelle, do you know how life just seems so hard sometimes?"

She: "Yes"

Me again: "And it seems to be the same thing over and over?"

She: "Yes"

Me: "And you just get so angry with God?"

She: "No."

Me: "No?"

She: "I cry sometimes. I go to Him and tell Him how much it hurts. But how could I get angry? He's the one who comforts me. And then I count my blessings."

Me (thinking, not speaking): *Counts her blessings? It sounds so simple, and—I don't know—almost dumb. How can you count your blessings in the face of children dying?*

But she meant it. And she did it. I just keep thinking of her every time one of those "over and over" things happens. She was a happy, peaceful woman. I learned from her to turn to God, not in anger, but with my pain. And to look around me at what is good in my life. There is always something.

I Needed This
July 24th

I needed reassurance that I am acceptable and loved. I opened my Scriptures and this popped up.

Casting all your cares upon him; for he careth for you.

1 Peter. 5:7 (King James Version)

A good reminder to me to look only to God for approval and strength.

The Lord's Formula for Joy In Trials
July 26th

I noticed lately I have been snacking—not feasting—on the words of Christ, and it is showing up in my attitude. I keep thinking I need to write a few experiences I've had with gratitude. I also need to spend the next few days just feasting on the Word until I'm centered again—which reminds me that one time it occurred to me that if I read the Scriptures more and ate less, I'd be healthier both spiritually and physically. I put my Scriptures in a plastic bag in the refrigerator and every time I opened the fridge to "just look" I read them. Enough of that. On to the Lord's formula for joy in trials.

When I was 28, I had five small children, one on the way and I was living in a two-bedroom house with only four other rooms: a living room, dining room, a small kitchen and a bathroom. I did day care for three other children in addition to my own. My first husband and I had bought the house, intending to fix it up. When we bought the house, our income was fine for the payments and a bit of remodeling. Thanks to sudden financial reverses, that changed.

We now had no money for fix up. Each day I would get up, look at my life and think, "Can it get any worse?" Five small children crammed into one tiny bedroom, extra small children around from 6 A.M. to 7 P.M. six days a week, no car, and constant financial struggles.

It could get worse, and did with a neighbor who was a little bit wacky. One day I looked out my kitchen window to see her spraying my two- year-old son with her garden hose. He was crying and trying to get away, but she just kept that spray on him until I called sharply out the window to her and headed out the back door. She was a strange one, and I was constantly on the lookout for what she was going to do next. It was hard to get away from her since her property L-shaped around ours.

I had a symbol of how bad my life was. It was the back

door. Every time I saw it, I thought of how I was suffering. It was originally a good wooden door with carvings that had been painted and repainted by previous owners. About seven layers of paint were on that door, which was all chipped and cracked. The latest color was yellow, but the chips showed green, white, pink, and, at one time red, underneath. Our plan had been to buy paint remover and sanding equipment and get that door back to its original wood. Two years later, we still could barely afford food and medical care on his new, much lower salary and my income from day care. The ugly, chipped yellow door was still there.

I could see it from almost every room in the house. A constant reminder of what seemed to be an impassable gap between my hopes, my goals, and the reality of my life.

One day as I was reading scriptures while simultaneously pouring out my heart to God, I read the Lord's formula for joy in trials, "Giving thanks for all things unto God and the Father in the name of Jesus Christ." Ephesians 5:20

I thought, *hmmm. Nothing here about receiving only the good things with thankfulness.* I thought about that yellow door. I decided to be thankful for it. I decided to be thankful for my symbol of all that was wrong with my life. I asked myself what I would do if I was really thankful for that yellow door. I decided I would take much better care of it. I scrubbed it down with a toothbrush and a cleaning paste until it shone bright and clean, even with all the chips and cracks. Now, every time I looked at that door I was reminded to look at my life and be thankful.

And not just for the good things. The real trick is learning to be thankful for the bad things—the struggles, the times of learning, the times I'm lost on the road. It isn't easy, but it is a commandment. One I've known the Lord to help me to keep by filling me with a sense of peace and contentment in the midst of trials when I turn to Him with a grateful heart.

Submission of the Will
July 27th

Been struggling with this once again. Today I started out just fine. Listening to and obeying the promptings and enjoying the peace that comes from it and noticing that I am immediately blessed, immediately! Even when I want it to be all about others, when I'm happy to make a seeming sacrifice, God slips in a blessing for me. He is so generous. For example, recently I felt I needed to visit Sister Charlene next time we were in Yosemite Park.

We're training for the Half Dome hike - a 20 mile challenge that takes being in good shape to make it up and back during day-light hours. I called Sister Charlene who lives in Yosemite Village to tell her we'd be making our second practice hike next Tuesday. I wondered if we could come visit. She was happy to have us come. Excited, actually. She was feeling just a wee bit Park-bound with the road closings due to flood damage.

When she found out I was planning to hike Half Dome the last Friday in September and was practicing for it, she invited us to stay in their spare bedroom the night before our Half Dome hike so we could get a good rest and an early start the next day. I was planning to camp up there and sleep on the ground the night before. Not my idea of restful sleep. She said, "Although, if you really want to camp, I'll understand if you turn us down." Right. I assured her I prefer a regular bed with a mattress.

See? I try to out give the Lord and just can't. Make His call, arrange a visit He knows is needed and I get a bed to sleep in the night before the Half Dome hike.

But once again, I got tired of listening halfway through the day and said, "Look. I have things I need to do. I'm going to ignore You for a while." I always regret it, and regret it now.

I felt impressed to make dinner early this morning, which I did, and then stored it in the fridge to reheat later. Prepared our Family Home Evening two days late. Then friends showed up at 4:30 this afternoon and *would not leave.* I went upstairs to get away from them for a minute and could feel the Spirit say, "This is why you made dinner early. It's all ready. Just invite them to stay and have family home evening with you." Do you remember this is how I first learned to recognize God speaking to me and how that gave our friends a prayed-for blessing? But I was completely rebellious.

"No!" I said. "I do not want company. I am sick of company. I just want You to make them leave."

But He didn't. They stayed until just before we had to leave for church. I never did invite them. Who knows what opportunities were missed?

As I sat down to read a little just before bed, I glanced over and here's the title of an article I felt prompted to read, "Insights From My Life" by Neal A. Maxwell.

Submission of the Will

The submission of one's will is the only uniquely personal thing we have to place on God's altar. It is a hard doctrine, but it is true. The other things we may give to God, however nice that may be of us, are actually things He has already given us, and He has loaned them to us . . . Our will . . . is the only possession we have that we can give, and there is no lessening of our agency as a result. Instead what we see is a flowering of our talents and more and more surges of joy. Submission to Him is the only form of submission that is completely safe . . .

Instead of choosing God and His ways, we get busy with the cares of the world, and that is when neighbors get excluded, too.

Ensign August 2000 p 9-10

It is such a struggle. I can't even keep it up for a whole day. I'm going to go get some sleep and start again tomorrow. Maybe I'll make it past noon.

Clearing Off the Desk
July 28th

Got an idea from Tom, the massage therapist, the other day. He said he had finally cleared up the clutter in his office. He had three and four foot piles of paper and magazines stacked all over his office and his desk. It's all neat and clean now. Thinking of my own cluttered work area, I asked how he had managed to accomplish that horrendous task.

He said he bought a shredder. Office clutter makes great garden compost.

I Will Lead Thee by the Hand
July 30th

I had this problem with money. After years and years of a life filled with constant financial downturns, I reached the point where I no longer believed we would ever be financially stable.

At one point, I could pray and feel that if I stayed on the path I was on, all would be well. But I no longer believed it. I had no faith in any promises concerning money. I felt I was in a catch-22 of faith. I was in the position of Peter walking on water to Christ. He loses faith and falls into the sea. *And immediately Jesus stretched forth his hand, and caught him, and said unto him, O thou of little faith, wherefore didst thou doubt ? Matthew 14:31*

"Well, yes," I said to the Lord. "But how do you overcome that? I have seen too many failures. I now cannot seem to overcome that fear no matter what I do, and thus no blessing and thus more fear. How do I stop this cycle? I need a way. Tell me the way, please."

And the Lord gave me a three-part program. This is a personalized program, so I'm not saying it will work for everyone, but going to the Lord does. My answer was to do these things daily for 90 days:

Repeat: The earth is full; there is enough and to spare.

Write a thank you note to a person who has made my life better.

Have dinner with my children.

Now, the first thing I did was to make a poster to track those things. Made a sign with those words on it. Got a box of thank you cards. Then I added a bunch of other things to my tracking poster. Hey, if I'm going to track things, might as well track it all. Drink two quarts of water daily, jog three times a week, balance my checkbook daily, and on and on.

After awhile, I noticed that the chart had lots of check marks, but not necessarily on the three things the Lord had given me. I was reminded only those three were important right now. Re-made the poster. Started on my 90 days again. Part of it was easy. I loved writing those letters. Although this ended up going on long enough that I was really reaching for people to write to. (Thank you, Miss Gravelly, for being my wonderful first grade teacher . . .)

The daily repetition was easy, too. My eyes were opened to the true fullness of the earth. There is life in every drop of water, in almost every bottle of "empty" air. Life and sources of food and energy that are often overlooked. I become entranced with the earth and all its life.

The dinners were a lot harder since I traveled often and my children were teenagers with sports and jobs and group project meetings.

I went to the Lord again. "Lord," I said. "Look at this. I'm having a hard time with those dinners. I have business trips. I have meetings and games to attend to watch my sons playing sports. What can I do?"

His answer was, "Have dinner with whomever is home."

"But," I said, "How about when I'm out of town? I just can't get that 90 days in a row. I keep starting and re-starting the count."

His answer? "I never said they had to be consecutive. You added that part."

Oh. Good news. It took me nine months to get those 90 days in. Said the scripture daily. Wrote the notes most of those days and finally had dinner together for 90 days.

Since then, I have never waked in the middle of the night in a cold sweat worrying about where the money for particular bills was going to come from. It always comes. I have always been able to handle it. The money will be there or the need for it will go away.

Twenty-four months ago, I realized I was having the same struggle with my weight. I no longer believed I could get it off. I prayed again. I said, "I am so busy. Is there some one key thing I can do for a particular time frame, like the money thing, and it will come off?" And His answer was, "Keep your desk cleared off for 180 days. No piles of things waiting to be done."

Keep my desk cleared? I've never had a completely clean desk top. Not even in grade school. But, I am getting there. It's taken eighteen months of work, and I am still not there yet. I had to think about it for six months.

In that eighteen months, in order to get my desk cleared, I have changed how I was making money, given up half the things that I was doing (and don't even miss doing), gone through every area of my home and storage areas and organized things, given up my own to-do lists and turned my life over to God and I am still working on it. I have about 10 days of a completely clean desk. But I am getting there. I know I will get there. But the changes I have had to make to get there are massive.

Do you think God has a sense of humor? "Just one thing, she asks. OK. Here's just one thing. Hahahahaha."

Maybe I should buy a shredder.

Grape Picking
August 31st

No, I'm not that hard up for money. Helping in the vineyard is part of the church welfare program which consists of multiple parts—helping people increase job skills, monthly fasting coupled with financial offerings to the welfare fund, spiritual growth of the people who need help *and* our own network of farms and canneries where we produce and store commodities for those in need. Most of the labor for the farms and canneries is provided by the members, generally unskilled volunteers.

I have worked in a hot, noisy cannery for hours doing backbreaking, tedious work and been grateful it's not my full-time job. I have peeled and cored tons of different kinds of fruit; planted and weeded potatoes, and now help with our raisin grape crop (you didn't really think we made wine, did you). Usually, this is all happening in 100 degrees, or hotter, heat. But this year, it is comparatively cool!

The work is hot, dirty and, in a way, fun. Little kids helping lay out paper, grandmoms picking bunches of grapes, teenagers picking and flirting. At the end, everyone is covered with sand and dust. The first year, I didn't know it was such a dirty job and wore white—white T-shirt, slacks and sandals. I never got any of it clean again.

Where did those ads for trips to Italy come from showing lovely peasant girls in peasant dresses, holding bunches of grapes? Probably the same place those ads showing women mopping those floors in heels came from. Now I know to wear old tennis shoes, old jeans and a black T-shirt.

Hard Physical Labor
September 21st

Last night we were short one counselor at our presidency meeting, as she was rolling grapes. What is that, you might ask? After we pick the grapes, we lay them on brown paper spread on the ground to dry into raisins. Then we go back and pick up the edges of the paper, rolling the grapes/raisins into the center of the paper. We roll the edges of the paper over to make a burrito wrap, fold the ends and fold the bundle in half to be picked up and dumped into a mechanical raisin-cleaning bin. That's "rolling grapes."

As I mentioned, we do this as part of the church welfare program. We all volunteer on different projects to provide food for others and ours is grapes/raisins. There are Mercedes and BMW's parked on the edges of the fields while everyone picks or rolls grapes. The rows are endless. You can't see one end from the other. At least a half mile of grapes per row, and we have two rows.

It is hard, backbreaking work. Or it would be, if you did it standing up and bending over the papers on the ground. I did not. The last time I went I sat, rolled grapes, and then scooted. It was still hot and tiring. I thought, *Thank you, God, that I am not an immigrant farm worker. I hate this. Then I thought, Great. This is not going to count as righteous serving on my part, because I'm doing it with such a bad attitude.* But I still hated it—the stooping, the squatting, the rolling and the lifting. I was sweaty and tired and achy. I decided younger, fitter people should do this. Definitely a good service project for the youth. At this point, is anyone in doubt about my position on hard, physical labor?

When it was too dark to see anymore, we left. Brother John—a man in his sixties who is not well and has many physical ailments—mentioned that he hadn't been able to get up once he got down. "So," he said cheerfully, "I just crawled from one paper to the next." I suddenly felt very ashamed of my complaining attitude . . . and deeply touched by the cheerful service that he so often gives while in terrible pain himself.

God-incidences
October 12th

I like this term for coincidences that aren't really coincidences. Yesterday, Parker and I were hurrying home from town when we made one last stop to have his watch band repaired. We like to go to this particular place, because the man takes such joy in working with watches. This is normally a 15-minute job that stretched into 45 minutes of frustration. Finally, it was done. The watch repairman charged us less than normal because it took so long. Lets you know what a good guy he is.

As we headed back home, we saw a car by the side of the road with a flat tire, the trunk open, an elderly man and a middle-aged woman nearby. Parker turned to me as he pulled over to help and said, "Oh, that's why it took so long to repair the watch."

Turned out to be people we knew. The woman said, "We didn't even have time to pray, and you're here already."

It gives us both a joy-jolt to be God's hands serving His children.

Be Of Good Cheer
October 18th

I cleared off my desk and rid my life of busyness. During my times of solitude, I notice I am sad, and often I weep. I realize I have been so busy that I haven't noticed how much sadness I have suppressed or ignored. I'm almost afraid to have time alone now.

Sunday, I knelt and prayed and told the Lord I was sad

and didn't know what to do about it. When I think about what I might be sad about, I come up with this list:

○ My poor actions in the past that affected other people adversely, especially my children.

○ My sins. Though I repented and changed my ways, it doesn't undo the damage already done.

○ The hurts I've endured myself because of other people's sins and cruelties.

○ The sickness of the world in which we live.

○ The anger and fighting and cruelties going on all around us. I do not see a solution. I trust that as the Bible promises this will lead to a time of peace, but even the Bible says it will get worse before it gets better. I do not see my path through these times.

As I prayed, this thought came to my mind, "Be of good cheer." Be of good cheer? What is this? God as Bobby McFarrin? Don't Worry, Be Happy. These are deep issues that bring sadness. And my answer is just "be of good cheer?" But I received no more. Just that.

I decided to look up the Scripture that had that in it. "Cheer" in the topical guide revealed the following:

Be of good cheer, thy sins are forgiven thee.

Matthew 9:2

Be of good cheer, it is I, be not afraid.

Matthew 14:27

In the world ye shall have tribulation, but be of good cheer, I have overcome the world.

John 16:33

Paul is beaten and thrown into prison, not knowing if he will live or die and receives this:

And the night following, the Lord stood by him and said, 'Be of good cheer, Paul, for as thou has testified of me in Jerusalem, so must thou bear witness also at Rome.'

Acts 23:11

Paul, to the sailors who are in danger of shipwreck says:

Be of good cheer for I believe God...
Acts 27:25

All of these promises were exactly suited to my sadness. When I am alone, and the sadness creeps up, I think of these words. And I do feel of good cheer.

Being A Witness
November 10th

I'm thinking of an experience I had in church last week. I usually go with a question and use that time for communing with the Lord. But this time I had no question. I opened my heart to any thought from Him. I received the impression that I am to be a witness. *What is that?* I wonder. I am reading Scriptures with the word "witness" in them.

Have You Noticed?
November 11th

Have you, too, noticed that when you let go of the anger, the sadness, and the pain that the joy is just there, waiting? It has been there all along.

Praying For My Adult Children
November 12th

All of my children are moved out now. Praying for my children is all I have left to do. All the training and advice-giving is over. Now is the time for only praying. Unless they unexpectedly call and ask for advice—which as they get closer to 30, they do more and more often. I have to admit that when it happens, I'm usually so stunned that it takes me awhile to think of any advice. Mostly, I just pray.

I pray that God will take care of their lives. That He will give them the circumstances and experiences they need that will lead them to Him. I pray that people will show up in their lives to guide and direct them when needed—people who will love them as much as I love them and to whom they will listen. They don't listen to me right now. Not while they are in their late teens and early twenties.

I tell them I am praying for them—even the ones who have rejected God and prayer. "I'm applying for this new job," one will say. "I will pray that if it's right for you, that you will get it," I answer.

"I hope the house closing goes smoothly," says another. "I will pray that it does," I answer. These declarations are usually met with silence. They worry that I will pressure them about God and religion. I don't, but I do speak what truth I know to them. And I am going to pray, and I tell them so.

"I can't keep up financially. My car keeps breaking. The rent's going up." "Pay your tithing," I say cheerfully. Truth is truth and I speak it. And they speak their truth back to me. "I don't believe in that stuff," they say. "OK," I say.

Occasionally, one actually does something I suggest. "I paid my tithing . . . and then got this bonus check for 'superior' work on a project. Do you believe it?" Of course, I do. The first time we pay tithing, the results are usually that quick. Later, it takes longer as we learn to budget, to find a better-paying position, to change our lives so we aren't always in trouble financially.

Occasionally I don't tell them I'm praying for them. I don't tell them I'm praying when I have a feeling it's going to take bad or painful experiences to turn the situation around. I learned this when I was praying once for Josiah. He had changed friends. I didn't trust his new friends—not all of them, just most. I prayed he would see them as they were. In a few months, he ended up in court twice thanks to incidents involving those friends—not serious stuff, just throwing-water-balloons-at-cars-kind-of-stuff. Most managed to get out of the situation, leaving Josiah holding the bag. One day, I was praying about these terrible things happening to Josiah when I felt the Spirit say, "This is the answer to your prayer."

"Get outta here!" I exclaimed. "I never prayed for anything like this." But then, I was reminded of that prayer. And Josiah did see those friends in a new light with no permanent damage done to him or his reputation. Now, at times, cautiously, I pray for whatever must happen either to them or me to make necessary changes.

I especially don't tell them when I'm praying against them. Matthias, for instance, knew he needed to get away from his Virginia friends. He kept saying, "God doesn't talk to me." And then he'd say, "I keep thinking I'd be better off in Denver." I prayed and prayed, because he knew what he should do, but wouldn't do it. It must have had an impact. Even his friends started telling him to go. "Go," they said. "When you're here, you skip class and skip work and waste your time."

I finally prayed that prayer – the one about letting whatever needed to happen happen to get him on the right path. Things did happen—bad things from Matthias's viewpoint. Off he went to Denver where he knew he should be.

I pray that God will open their eyes so that they will see His hand in their lives. Matthias's car died on the way to Denver. Threw a rod right at an exit outside of St. Louis. His Aunt Cara, unknown to either of us, just happened to be in St. Louis that weekend and was on her way back to Denver that very day. Reached by cell phone, she stopped to pick up Matthias and bring him with her to Denver.

Matthias is not foolish enough to think this is a coincidence. While angry that his car died, the timing is just too perfect even for him to ignore. "The car died right at an exit. The service station man said he couldn't believe I was able to drive it as far as I did. And Aunt Cara was right there to pick me up! I know it was God looking out for me."

I can tell their hearts are starting to soften when they

start asking me to pray for them. "I don't pray," they say. "But will you pray for me? Will you fast for me?"

"Of course," I say. "Of course." We'll take this one step at a time.

It Just Takes Time
November 13th

I am learning patience in this calling as Relief Society president—patience *and* perseverance. Last week, I finally saw the result of a year and a half of constant, almost daily effort, to change hearts. Not a complete change of hearts, but at least, a start.

Sister Geneva—the star of my first entry, "The Room," is beginning to change her melancholy attitude toward life. "You know what I realized?" she asked me last week just before a friend's funeral. "I'm happiest when I'm serving other people."

You think so? I thought, but was wise enough not to say. I beamed a quick prayer to God, "I think your plan might actually be working!"

You think so? I suspect He thought, but was kind enough not to say.

I spent a year and a half serving Sister Geneva, concerned about her depression and unhappiness after her husband died. *She needs to serve,* I thought. *She needs a friend. She and Sister Larue would be good for each other.*

I worked to help Sister Geneva see her need for service and to get her together with Sister Larue. She just wasn't getting it. And neither was Sister Larue, complaining because her best friend had gone on a mission. "I need my friend here," she'd said emphatically.

"Maybe you could call Sister Geneva and arrange an activity together," I said.

"No. I don't know her very well," Sister Larue said.

(That's the point. I want to snap at her but don't. Make her your friend.)

I called Sister Geneva every chance I had, not only to offer help, but also to give her service projects. Over and over I asked, "Will you take a meal here, please? We could use help with these quilts, please. Will you go with me to drop food here, or help clean this house or do laundry for this woman who is ill?" I especially pushed her to go when Sister Larue needed help after her two hospitalizations and her major illness.

Every time she helped, she was happier for a while. Often she couldn't go, as she was scheduled to be at another activity with one of her many friends; although she seemed unaware of just how busy and involved she was. I would call at 10 A.M. and she would answer, sounding sleepy and tired. "I just don't feel like getting up," she'd say. "I'm just too sad. I didn't sleep well last night, and now I don't feel like getting up. I just sit here all alone, day after day. No one cares or calls or comes by."

"I've been calling for three days, but you never answer," I'd say.

"Oh, I went shopping with so and so yesterday, and the day before that there was a big project over at the senior center, and then at the first of the week, a friend wanted me to come spend the day with her," she said, never acknowledging the disparity between her complaint about being ignored and her obviously active life.

"Where I used to live, people called all the time," Sister Geneva said "I think the people in this church are very unfriendly and uncaring."

I said, "I'm sorry if I've neglected you, but we have three people in the hospital for emergency surgery, and another two who need help packing and cleaning as they are moving."

"Oh, I didn't *know that*," she said, her mood immediately changing. "What can I do to help?" She is a great one for service. When she knows there's a need, she can be counted on to help. So I knew all I had to do was mention a need, and she'd leap to fill it.

From time to time—more times than could possibly be coincidence—she'd complain about being ignored by a specific person. "That person is seriously ill right now," I'd say.

"Oh, I didn't *know that,*" she'd say. Once again, her mood immediately changing. "What can I do to help?"

Other times the conversation went like this: "I don't understand why I'm still here. I have no reason to still be alive. Why don't I just die?"—the lament of many older people who have seen husbands, parents, brothers, sisters and good friends all pass away, leaving only them.

"You must still have something to learn," I'd say. And she'd laugh—her saving grace. She always does pick up quickly on the underlying humor when we speak. And then she'd say, "Well I'm ready to learn it. Just tell me what it is."

"How about going with me to take food to so and so?" I'd ask, giving her a small hint. "Why can't we just tell her?" I'd ask God, wanting to say sharply to her, "You're always happiest when you help others. Stop sitting around feeling sorry for yourself. Get out there and look for people you can help." But God reminded me that that's not my job. At times, she seemed such a burden to me—an unchanging load of sadness and sorrow.

I would stand by the phone as her caller ID came up, dreading the sound of her high pitched needy voice and count the rings as I tried to convince myself to pick it up, just pick it up. But oh how I did not want to. I always did though.

And then, an odd thing happened. I fell in love with her. We always end up laughing when we're together. I'm such an egotist I can't help but love a person who gets my humor. I look forward to spending time with her. At a friend's funeral, she introduced me to people as her mother; because, she said, "Margaret always comes when I need her." We laughed at my 50-year-old self being her 83-year-old self's mother.

I began to understand why she was having such a hard time with this. Most of us make decisions about how life is when we are very young. Sister Geneva's youth was hard and painful – her father murdered before her young eyes, left orphaned and badly burned as a pre-schooler, sent to live with an austere strict uncle. Eighty-three years old and she continues to struggle with depression.

Then last week I got these two calls. The first from Sister Geneva: "You know something? I'm happiest when I'm serving others." Next Sister Larue called, "Do you know Sister Geneva needs a friend?"

"Does she?" I say.

"Yes," says Sister Larue firmly. "I want you to make her my visiting teaching companion, so that we can spend more time together."

"Good idea," I say, glancing heavenward once again.

Thank you, God, for letting me be Your partner.

Conversation with Sisters Geneva and Larue
November 23rd

After I finished editing the journal entries for this book, I called Sisters Geneva and Larue. "Come, let me treat you to an ice cream cone," I said. "I have written a book, and you are in it. I want you to hear it first. I'm concerned you might be offended."

I started reading "The Church Grandmother" to them. Sister Larue said, "Am I the church grandmother? I don't want to be that."

"Oooh," I said. "It gets worse than *that*." I kept reading. When I finished they said, "We sound like crabby old ladies."

"I know," I said. "And you aren't. I have lots of entries in my journal that point out how fun you are, but these are the ones God wanted in here. Don't blame me," I finish my defense, sounding like a little kid, "Blame God."

This is to tell you that they really are funny ladies. One entry in my journal that didn't make it in here describes a night of cookie making with Sister Geneva and the Sister Nell. I had to leave for two hours and fully expected to come back to find the job finished. They had not baked *one cookie* in that entire two hours! They were just laughing and talking the whole time I was gone.

Sister Geneva is a wonderful cook. She invites us to dinners where she serves incredibly delicious meals with beautifully set tables. She now shares that talent with the women of the church by being in charge of refreshments on Enrichment Night.

Sister Larue has enough energy for four people. She has to have many friends, because no one friend can keep up with her. I can't imagine what she was like at 30 if she's slowed down, as most people do as they get older.

We took a Readers Theatre class together and put on a couple of well-received plays—the best in the class, and that's no exaggeration. We did a reading from *The Wind in the Willows* where she was Badger and I was Toad. She sounds and moves exactly like you imagine Badger sounding and moving; I told her it was typecasting. The class loved it.

But the best thing about Sister Geneva and Sister Larue is that they are servers. They can both be counted on to help when help is needed.

I Am the Moon
November 24th

I am the moon, I say, because all my light is a reflection of the Son.

Back to Being an Apprentice
December 1st

I am sitting here, happily listening to peaceful music

and waiting until time to give massages. I am just enjoying the peace. And then I start crying. Why? Is it as experts have suggested that I don't feel worthy to enjoy this?

It is.

I can't think of any happy, peaceful days when my children were small—just days filled with money worries and food worries, and my impatience and irritability as a result. Is this so? Were there no happy, peaceful days?

I kneel to pray and sob. What right do I have to be so happy now when I was so impatient with my many young ones then? Or even ignored them completely? And the answer from God to my heart: There were happy days. I wasn't always impatient.And none of it matters anyway. It´s past. What matters is now.

Where is joy? Joy is in loving God and man. Go forward now in peace. I am filled with gratitude for my life as it is today—this very day, sitting on my massage table in my little seven-by-twelve foot room with one wall still needing paint. Listening to gentle, peaceful music. Listening and looking forward to going home to see the children and grandchildren in fewer than two weeks.Listening and enjoying Parker and our lives together each day. Listening and enjoying just being able to serve every day in some way. I pick up my Scriptures. I read a verse this morning that I think fits this mood. I want to write it. As I lift the already opened book, a different scripture leaps out at me:

Daughter, be of good comfort. Thy faith hath made thee whole. And the woman was made whole from that very hour.

Matthew 5:22

Thank you, God. How can I best spend today?

"Feed my sheep."

And who needs feeding, today? Here´s the list He gave me. Not even a very long one. Only six people. Two I will be giving massages for and talking with. Three to call. And the missionaries to feed (literally). But I am impressed with the thought that they are a little discouraged and need my faith and support to shore them up. They are young and far from home, and it is the holiday season.

Back to being an apprentice. I love it. I love serving hand in hand with God.

Out the Door
December 5th

I have to leave for out-of-town training today. I sat down with Parker three days ago and said, "Parker. We have nine days before we leave town for two weeks. Eight of the nine days are filled. I am doing out-of-town training for three of those days, the Santa's Workshop and the Christmas party for the church is one of those days. Two of those days are Sundays, and one day we are going to the big city to go shopping for our business supplies. One day we have to be witnesses in court. There are no days left. I have to fit cleaning, packing and visiting teaching all in, in the cracks. Please *don't add anything.*"

He said, "I won't." We went to visit a friend who needed our help that night. While we were there, Parker invited them to dinner Friday night. ARGH! We leave early the following Wednesday for our cross-country trip. Parker assures me we *needed* to invite these people. I am reminded that serving is not always convenient.

Gifts
December 14th

A surprise party from God! Our lesson on Sunday was on gifts from the Savior and from God. It was almost routine. The teacher was asking the standard questions, "What are we doing with our gifts? Do we recognize the gifts we have been given?

As an object lesson and discussion starter, the teacher passed around a basketful of scrolls, each with a gift written on it, hidden inside the scroll. We each randomly chose one or two scrolls without opening them until they were all taken. We then opened and read them

The veterinarian's wife—a dog trainer—opened hers to "Love of animals." The professional singer had chosen, "Love of music." The stay-at-home mother of eight who was living on a park ranger's salary found "creativity" and "frugality."

It continued for 25 women. The room became quieter and quieter as we listened to each sister open her scroll and read her gift. We realized the Spirit of God had stepped in and given us a special one-of-a-kind, this-Sunday-only gift. Each random choice had been directed by a Godly hand. We felt the Spirit confirm that these gifts were indeed the ones we had been given by God. The room was filled with love and gratitude to God for our gifts and for each other.

The Dogs
December 15th

We're visiting my sister Cara as part of this Christmas trip. Last night as my sister was finally sitting down at 8 P.M.—after running five children to various practices, recitals and doing all the other things that mothers of five do—she said, "Let the dogs in." The dogs?

In bounded two long and lanky puppies as wild and exuberant as you would expect after being left alone all day. She does not have time for dogs. There is no one home to train the dogs.

"Why do you have these dogs," I ask. "Where did these dogs come from?"

"We have these dogs," she says with a look, "Because

your son found six abandoned puppies by the side of the road, and these are the last two."

Oh. Matthias strikes again. (Of course he can't keep them; he lives in an apartment. She lives in a 3,500-square-foot house on 2.25 acres.)

Lost Keys
December 24th

I lost my keys last night. Not unusual for me. I was positive I'd laid them on the bed with my wallet in my niece's room where we're staying. She had piled some clean laundry on the bed after I laid the wallet and keys down. I looked under the clothes—found the wallet but no keys. I looked next to the bed, on the bedside tables, and under the bed. No keys. Not on the kitchen counter, not in the car, not in the suitcases, not near the computer, not even in our coat pockets. I went back in with Parker and picked up every piece of clothing on the bed. Looked in every place again—no keys.

Everyone was searching for them. We were getting desperate. We only had the one set with us. Finally, I stopped for a moment with Zack my seven-year-old grandson nearby and said, "I'm going to pray to find them."

After a few seconds of silence, Zack said, "I thought you were going to pray."

"I am," I said. "I'm praying in my heart. God can hear you when you pray in your heart."

He was silent for a few moments, too. Then he said, "Do you think God heard me?"

I was touched. "Did you pray for my keys?" I asked.

"No, I prayed for some more Jolly Ranchers™ candy," he said. "There's none in any of the candy bowls, and Great-grandma Betty says she doesn't have anymore."

I snorted. "I'm sure He heard, Zack, but I doubt that God answers candy prayers."

We continued to look – repeatedly looking in places we'd already searched. Twice Parker and I went back to the bed sorting through, folding and searching the clothing. We split up again and looked under chairs, between couch cushions feeling more and more desperate.

After another half hour Parker came up to me carrying a flashlight and acting in that agitated way he acts when he's feeling inspired. He insisted we look outside again. We could see our footprints in the freshly fallen snow. We walked in the dark, swinging the flashlight from side to side along the footprints, even checking under the nearby shrubbery.

Following the footprints all the way to the car, then walking around and looking under and in the car, we still could find no keys. I was so sure Parker was on the right track when he was acting in that agitated way. Then without warning, Parker headed off onto the front lawn. I asked why he was looking there. He could see we hadn't walked there. Did he think I'd taken the keys and tossed them up onto the lawn, then forgotten I'd done that? He ignored my comments and kept looking around on the snow-covered lawn anyway. Suddenly, he stopped and started digging a bit in the snow... sure enough, guess what he found?

A half dozen Jolly Ranchers candies, still in their wrappers. "Hey, God did hear my prayer! Here's my candy God sent me," said Zack.

Later we found the keys in the bedroom on the bed under that same laundry Parker and I had both carefully checked. I guess God wanted Zack, and me, to learn that there are times He does answer candy prayers.

Ten Minutes
January 20th

Just before we left for our trip to the auction on Tuesday (yes, another trip), I realized I had not been going to the Lord for my daily errand, because I was so busy. I decided I couldn't live like this any longer. I needed my relationship with God. I needed to know that He knows how grateful I am for all He's given me and how willing I am to be of service. It was 7:45 A.M. and we had to leave at 8:00 A.M. There would be no free time for the rest of the day. We were leaving that night and would be gone for two days. I had 10 whole minutes.

I knelt and said, "I have ten minutes before we have to leave. Is there anything I can do?"

And the answer was yes. The impression in my mind was immediate. Call Sister Janice. I did. I listened to her for ten minutes. Then, when I told her I had to go, she said, "Thank you so much for calling. I really just needed someone to talk with today. You have no idea how much this meant to me to have you call right now."

I like to give credit where credit is due. It wasn't me, you know. It was God. He can use even 10 minutes, if that's all you have to give.

Dump the Deadbeats
January 21st

That's what I said early in December as we planned presidency lessons for January. I even had Scriptures to back me up: the story of Gideon and his army in the Old Testament. The Israelites are going to war against the Midianites, and God says that Gideon doesn't need all the Israelites. Says if there are too many, they'll start thinking they won because of their own strength and not because of God. (Such a standard human reaction to pray for a blessing, get it, then decide it isn't God after all.)

Send home the ones who are afraid or fearful, God instructs Gideon. Twenty-two thousand leave with 10,000 remaining. "Still too many," says God. A little test was devised, and all except 300 were sent home. That 300 defeated an army that is described this way, "The children of the east lay along in the valley like grasshoppers for multitude; and their camels were without number as the sand at the seaside." Gideon defeats this army. If you want to know how, read Judges Chapter 7, because how he did it isn't the point of this entry.

"The point is," I say to my counselors, "if the sisters aren't going to fulfill their callings, especially visiting teaching, we're dumping them. God can accomplish His work without them. He will multiply the efforts of those of us who *will* do the work as He did the loaves and the fishes, and all will be filled."

They said to me, "Um. You aren't going to say it quite like that are you?"

"Thinking of it," I say. "Just exactly like that."

I'm going to tell the Gideon story, and then tell them how it applies. They can either come along, do the job, and be part of God's work, or they can be left behind. I'm tired of coddling them and begging them and encouraging them. Either do it or you're out. Got it?!

"In addition," I say, "if this one Relief Society teacher comes up with another excuse for not teaching in December, we're releasing her and getting a sister who will do the job."

One counselor asks to give the Gideon story before I tell the sisters how it applies. I said OK. She prepared the story along with a little visual aid.

December has come and gone. The sister who keeps missing on the Sundays she is to teach showed up to teach in December.

But the visiting teaching is still being ignored by quite a few. While I was listening to the the church service meeting talk today, it occurred to me that maybe God didn't want me dumping these people. I'm not the One who called them. We prayed, and God said He wanted them called. What makes me think I can just release them without His permission or His direction?

"Well," I say, "they aren't doing the job. They haven't learned to trust You and just do the job and know You will handle the rest for them. And they aren't listening when we tell them You will." Not my problem, the Spirit reminds me. My job is to listen, encourage, and love.

Church is over and we're now having our Relief Society lesson. The sister I'd considered releasing is teaching. She tells us a story. During December she had been through a trying time with her preschool-aged son the week prior to her turn to teach. He had not been able to eat anything all week, had been in and out of the doctor's office, was on the verge of dehydration, and potentially needed to be hospitalized.

She hadn't wanted to teach that December Sunday, but after much prayer, felt the Lord's assurance that if she showed up and fulfilled her calling, that she and her family would be blessed for it. Her husband came to the church service as he was on the program, then went home and took over the sick boy while she came to church to teach our women's class. She says when she got back home from teaching her lesson, her husband told her that at 12:30 P.M. the young boy jumped up out of the chair where he'd been laying lethargically all week, said he was hungry, ate a <u>lot</u> of food and then went out to play. The child was happily playing as she came home, and has been fine since.

She knew now that if she did what God wanted her to do, that she and her family would be taken care of. She had started teaching at 12:30 P.M.

Hmmm, I think to myself, feeling very humbled and repentant. *I guess God doesn't need me to teach them these lessons. He does it much more effectively than I can.*

I am reminded that my calling is to minister, not to AD-minister. And for sure, not to judge, condemn or speak my mind. The counselor then gives the lesson for which we had set aside time. As she started, she said that she had felt prompted to change it completely during church service. She wasn't sure how to change it, she said, until she heard this sister's story about her young son. She did not give the Gideon story. As she ended, I looked at her and said, "No Gideon story?"

She looked back at me, "No. No Gideon story."

Thank you, God, for counselors who listen to You and not to me.

The Holy Spirit
January 22nd

Yesterday in the Bible study class, I noticed we had a visitor. I thought for a minute that if I were teaching I might be a little nervous in front of a visitor. Then I thought, *What if it was Billy Graham? Or the Pope?*

Then I thought, *What if I had brought a <u>quote</u> from Billy Graham or the Pope that I planned to read? I might start worrying about whether it actually was a quote from him. Where had I gotten it anyway? And is it exactly as he said it?* As I read it, I'd probably look at him to see if he was nodding in agreement that those were his words.

Another thought. *What <u>if God the Father and Jesus Christ were here</u> and I was the teacher? I'd be worried about my whole lesson.*

And then I realized that's exactly what happens every week. When I teach the true principles of the Gospel, the Holy Ghost or Spirit is there confirming it in our hearts. That's what we mean when we say, "The Spirit was here." Exactly as if God or Christ were sitting there nodding, saying "Yes. That's what I said. That is the truth."

Now I understand why it's important to use scriptures and to quote them exactly, not paraphrase them. That is my obligation as a teacher – to teach the true doctrine by the Spirit, not my own *"philosophy and vain deceit, after the tradition of men." Col 2:8*

Death Surrounds Me
February 9th

Once again I sit in a hospital room, watching her watch him. He is unconscious, on a respirator. It is the Intensive Care Unit (ICU.) No distractions. Just the machines and me. Watching her watching him. A woman in her seventies watching her husband of decades.

She looks happy to see me when I come in. I know the prognosis is not good. I know when Brother John and Parker gave him a blessing using oil and the laying on of hands they both felt he would not survive this. But Brother John felt he would rally for a while. Long enough to make amends with those members of his family he has not yet contacted.

Parker told me Brother John took her aside and told her, "You must see that this happens. That is why he will recover. Don't waste this time. You must be the strong one. You will see a recovery," he says, "But probably not enough to come home."

She said, unable to hear the truth, "Yes. I am looking forward to when he comes home." She didn't understand.

Now, two days later I am sitting with her as she watches the machines. She tells me, "Brother John told me he will recover and come home."

I know that is not what was said. But if she could not hear him, I doubt she will hear me.

I remember a similar experience as we watched my father die. We listened as the hospice worker described the final stages of dying to us as we gathered around my father in his bedroom—the slowing of the breaths, the last long deep exhalation. Afterward, I could see it had all happened just as she described it. But I couldn't see while it was happening. We thought we had a few more days, not a few more minutes. We could not see it. She cannot hear it.

She stays in a recreational vehicle (RV) in the Walmart parking lot, rather than make the hour and a half commute from this hospital to our little rural town. During the day she watches him breathe. Nothing to distract her. No television, no telephone. This is ICU. She watches the readouts on the machines that faithfully note each small change.

"Look" she says to me, "This morning his blood pressure was 185/92. Now it's 175/90. That's much better." I nod my head. Not in agreement, but in acceptance of her wishes for it to be so. She will see when she is ready.

She stays until she must leave. Then she goes home to her RV in the Walmart parking lot. I see those RV's in a new way now. Wondering what might be behind those small windows tightly shuttered.

The Coolness of Logic
February 10th

Today I am to sit with Sister Kay in ICU. She is in her 30's. Her husband's life eroding as he moves from one crisis to the next, each time recovering less and less function. Heart attack, loss of one kidney, the other barely functioning, massive infection in his lungs that spread to his blood. Is this the last crisis? There is panic in her voice when we speak, and tears in her eyes as we arrange meals and rides for her children.

I rose at 5:30 this morning to create simple reports in Access™ for a client. The house was quiet. The only sound was that of the keyboard responding to my fingers. Even the constant chatter of anguished inner voices were stilled by the cool power of logic. Clear black letters and lines laid out on a white background. As the report prints, each line follows the other neatly down the page, each field in order, correctly spaced from the one before. No emotion. No conversation. Crisp lines of type requiring only logic to lay it out and run it.

There is an occasional odd result that requires a deeper dive into reason and intellect. I embrace that dive as I would a dive into cool, clear water allowing me to enter a world of silence, calmness, clarity, absence of emotion.

This isn't what I expected when I was called to serve as Relief Society president. This empathic pain. This need for solace that I see so clearly only He can provide. I step aside for a while, needing a break before I take up this burden once more.

Another Widow
February 28th

Another man from church died unexpectedly Sunday. He and his wife retired ten years ago after his quadruple bypass and spent all their time doing things they enjoyed together - trips to Europe and China and five months RV'ing across America. Then settled here near the children and grandchildren. They were just walking around their property planning what trees to plant where, how to finish off the drive, when he said he felt dizzy and went down.

I went to see his wife on Monday. She said, "We'd been together 51 years. We were inseparable." She looked too young to have been married 51 years. I suppose I looked surprised, because she said, "I married him when I was 16."

"How did you meet him?"

"At church. I wasn't allowed to date until I was 16, but my mom talked my dad into letting me date him, even though I was only 15 and he was a sailor. She told my dad he was a good man. My dad cried when I wanted to marry him right after I turned 16. He was being transferred and I wanted to go with him. They didn't want me to, but they knew how headstrong I was and didn't argue with me."

"Looks like it worked out," I said thinking of those 51 years.

She laughed. "We made a good team," she said, "Everyone said that. But that doesn't mean we didn't fight. We fought. We yelled. Well, I yelled. He was always quiet. He just listened, and you'd think he was agreeing, and then he went and did whatever he wanted. He always did exactly what he wanted." She laughed thinking about it. "I just was thinking last week that we're still fighting about the same things now that we fought about the first week we got married. But we didn't ever mention divorce. Not once."

"You just fought it out," I said.

"We just fought it out," she agreed. "We didn't hold grudges." A pause. "He was the only man I ever even kissed."

Tonight I'm on the phone getting commitments from the sisters for casseroles, salads and desserts to feed a hundred after a Thursday funeral. It doesn't seem like enough to show in what high honor I hold that fifty-one year relationship.

Guilt - Why I Like It
March 4th

First, a word about judging. People always misquote the judgment scripture. It actually says in John 7:24, "Judge not according to the appearance, but judge *righteous* judgment."

We must judge other people. How else do we decide whom to marry or whom to trust? The question is how do we learn to judge righteously? First, we must learn to recognize righteousness. This is where guilt comes in and why I like guilt. I bring this up because guilt has gotten a bad reputation lately. People want to do away with it. I like guilt for the same reason I like pain. Guilt is to the spirit as pain is to the body. And joy is to the spirit as pleasure is to the body.

As a modern society, we've decided to keep joy and throw out guilt. Is that even possible? If you got rid of your nerve endings so you wouldn't feel pain, could you then feel pleasure? Is it good not to feel pain? What if we couldn't?

Imagine trying to convince a two year old not to touch a hot stove if he felt no pain. Do you think he might leave his hand on the stove sometime when you weren't looking and cause serious damage to his body?

There are diseases where people lose feeling and do not have pain. Leprosy is one such disease. People who have it must constantly be on the watch for injuries that most of us would notice immediately. Injuries that are worse than they would be if they could have felt the pain that accompanies it. Injuries that often become infected, leading to loss of a limb.

Pain is good. It alerts us to injuries or sicknesses. It keeps us from badly injuring ourselves physically. Guilt does the same for the spirit.

Can we become insensitive to it? Sure. People who have trained themselves not to feel guilt are spiritual lepers.

Isn't guilt just an outmoded vestige of puritanical teachings? Aren't we born as blank slates that our culture writes on? That was the argument that one of the first anthropologists Margaret Mead was trying to prove. But over and over anthropologists, historians and other students of humanity consistently found a core group of taboos in societies suggesting that we are born with an innate sense of right and wrong, suggesting we are *not* blank slates at birth.

This core set is then added to and expanded upon by the culture. The core set has taboos against lying, stealing, murdering or committing sexual immorality and, on the positive side, emphasizes recognizing a God, honoring our family, and learning to love and forgive.

To try to prove the blank slate theory, Margaret Mead was looking for a culture that did not have this core set. The whole point of the book Coming of Age in Samoa was to say that at last we found a culture without sexual taboos. But it was a lie. They hadn't found such a culture. That Samoan culture had a very strong set of taboos against pre- and extramarital sex, just as did all others until today.

The truth is that we are all born with this innate sense of right and wrong. Why else tell a small child that if any one touches him in a way that makes him feel bad or "uncomfortable," he should come and tell you? What is that "uncomfortable" or bad feeling we expect he'll have, if not an innate sense of knowing right from wrong.

In the Christian world this innate sense of knowing right from wrong is called our conscience. It is also known as the light of Christ. The chief passage in the New Testament is found in Romans 2: 14-15. *For when the Gentiles, which have not the law, do by nature the things contained in the law, ... their conscience also bearing witness.* The concept is that we are born with a natural capacity to distinguish between right and wrong regardless of race, religion or nationality.

The possession of this ability at once makes us responsible beings. We cannot blame society for not teaching us right and wrong. We innately know when a deed or attitude is wrong.

What does guilt feel like? It feels like how you feel after you've just said something rude to a person who didn't deserve it, or you took that item from work that you hope no one finds out about. It feels bad. It causes feelings of depression and anger. It is the opposite of joy.

What's the appropriate response to guilt? It is the same as the appropriate response to pain. Take my hand off the hot stove. Stop doing the thing that makes me feel guilty. Clean up the burn or the mess I've made.

It isn't society's or the church's or my parent's fault that I guilty. I feel guilty because I should. I'm grateful for it. It lets me know I need to quit doing that thing, whatever it is, and go for the joy of a peaceful spirit.

How can we train this ability? By paying attention to the twinges. By reading the Scriptures and praying so that we learn how to love and act righteously. We can look back through our life to see where we might have initially felt guilt, but then convinced ourselves it didn't matter until we became deadened to it. We re-awaken our sensitivity to guilt. We learn to discern between truth and error, between righteousness which leads to eternal life and joy, and unrighteousness which leads to eternal death.

As we learn to discern truth and righteousness in ourselves, we are then able to judge righteously. As we judge righteously, we make good choices and have lives of peace and joy. That's why I like guilt. It leads us to God and to peace and to joy.

Position Open
March 5th

Michael said he doesn't like disciplining his child. She just turned two and is being quite the little rebel. He said, "I wish I could hire a punisher, then I could just be the good guy all the time."

I didn't think to tell him his consistent firmness only deepens her love for him.

Being Where I'm Needed
March 12th

Another funeral today. The husband of the woman who parked her RV in Walmart died recently. He is also the father of Brother Mike who inspired my "Raising Boys" entry. Mike's father was buried in our small town cemetery. It looks as if the neighbor donated part of his field to the town for the cemetery. There's a barn just on the other side of the cemetery fence. A cow was mooing during the graveside service. There are trees throughout the field. Every grave is near a tree. It's small. This is the green time of year in California that flowers are blooming. The green hills and valleys surround us, creating a quiet feeling of peace and well-being—one small moment of peace in an otherwise busy, frantic day.

No. There was one other moment of perfect stillness in this busy, busy day. It happened like this. It was the kind of day where all the little details were going wrong rather than coming together. The sister with the tablecloths for the food-serving tables forgot to bring them. She lives half an hour from the chapel. With limited time we called a sister who lives closer, but she was at work.

"The house is open," the sister with the tablecloths said. "Just get them out of the linen closet." I hurried to find Parker and the car keys. Instead of Parker and the keys, I found three sopranos, 2 basses and 2 tenors in need of an alto to sing for the service. I am an alto, and I was there. I guess that meant I was to do it. Another sister handled the finding of tablecloths while I practiced singing with less than an hour to go before the start of the service. In between verses I gave directions to the sisters who were bringing food.

Finally, the eye of the storm—the family gathered in the Relief Society room for family prayer and a last moment alone with their father/husband/brother before the casket was closed. Parker and I were invited, but he was nowhere to be seen. I went in alone. We talked for a few minutes about what it had been like growing up in their home as siblings with their dad in charge. How he and his wife had met. At last we gave up on Parker and just went ahead without him. After the family prayer, the family left and left the job of closing the casket to Brother Mike. He wanted to put on a cap with special meaning to his father before closing the casket. I knew Brother Mike was going to need help for this one last act and thought Parker should be there to help, but he wasn't. *Someone should be here,* I thought as everyone filed out.

I stayed. I thought it would be better if his wife or one of his brothers was there. Or Parker, who had helped dress his father in the funeral home. I stepped twice to the door to call someone, anyone back, but the hallway was empty. I tried to leave to find Parker, but was constrained by the Spirit. I had a sense of there not being enough time. He needed a helper and, like the need for an alto, I was available. I stayed.

Brother Mike tried and tried to put on cap by himself,

but just couldn't handle it. It was breath-holding quiet in this room that just minutes before had been filled with family. Incredible stillness. No sound, not even from the hallway. As if we were caught in a time-warp.

Finally, as he continued to struggle, I stepped over and gave assistance. He said, "Good-bye, Dad. I love you. I'll miss you." And then turned to me, put his arms around me, his head on my shoulder and sobbed while I held him. He said, "Why did it have to be you standing here?"

I don't know, I was wondering that myself. I was calm and at peace at the time, but I'm left with that uneasy, nervous feeling I get when I've been involved in too intimate a moment. I want to go to God and say, "I'm not really the right person for this job. Maybe you should get someone else." Is anyone the right person for this job?

God Wants To Talk With Me
May 1st

I think God wants to talk with me. It has been months since I have had serious study and reflection time. It's going to take more than one scripture. I must listen. I am to ask, and the Lord will answer. I ask, "What are Your words to me today?"

Woe unto him that striveth with his Maker ! Let the potsherd strive with the potsherds of the earth. Shall the clay say to him that fashioneth it, what makest Thou? or thy work, He hath no hands?

Isaiah 45 9

God created man and the world; therefore, He commands and it obeys. I am not to counsel God, but to obey Him. What am I being asked to do? "See the sacredness in all of God's children. Bring My healing to them."

What man of you, having an hundred sheep, if he lose

one of them, doth not leave the ninety and nine in the wilderness, and go after that which is lost , until he find it? And when he hath found it, he layeth it on his shoulders, rejoicing. And when he cometh home, he calleth together his friends and neighbours, saying unto them, Rejoice with me; for I have found my sheep which was lost . I say unto you, that likewise joy shall be in heaven over one sinner that repenteth, more than over ninety and nine just persons, which need no repentance.

Luke 15:4-7

Surely he hath borne our griefs, and carried our sorrows: yet we did esteem him stricken , smitten of God, and afflicted . But he was wounded for our transgressions, he was bruised for our iniquities: the chastisement of our peace was upon him; and with his stripes we are healed .

Isaiah 53:4-5

A Reminder
May 10th

Unexpected visitors showed up cutting my study time short Wednesday morning. Still, the little I read was a forceful reminder. I read in Luke 22:31-32, "The Lord said, 'Simon, Simon, behold, Satan hath desired to have you, that he may sift you as wheat; But I have prayed for thee, that thy faith fail not ...'"

I am reminded that my prayers are needed on behalf of myself, my friends and my children. I am reminded that prayer is a power and the prayers of the faithful are honored—they are a protection for those we love.

Micromanagement
May 24th

Insight! Insight! I'm having a hard time praying for my daily task, because I don't like being micromanaged. I want to hear a command such as "Go thou and preach 'repent or be destroyed to the Ninevites'," and then I get left alone for a month or more to accomplish it. This daily and hourly thing is getting on my nerves.

I'm going to go pray about it and see what we can work out.

Because Thou Hast Not Murmured
June 17th

I have been struggling with two things: how to *want* to do the Lord's will each day and how to stay positive in the face of constant defeat.

When I consider that Susan B. Anthony never did see women get the right to vote in her lifetime and when I read that Samuel Garrison published "The Liberator" for 35 years before the Emancipation Proclamation became law, I wonder how one fights such a fight without becoming bitter and discouraged and angry and frustrated. I don't like those emotions. I wonder what the secret is to remaining joyful and firm and committed in the face of constant defeat and setbacks.

I once again have been ignoring my prayers. Not going to the Lord because I have things I want to do. As many times as I have been blessed by following His will; as many times as I have made the call or visit I was prompted to make only to learn how desperately it was needed; as often as I have felt the joy of serving at that time, I still want to live my life *my way*.

In an effort to remind myself of my calling to serve, I posted a picture of Christ as a shepherd on the front of my diary and on my desktop. It reminds me of Christ's statement to Simon Peter in John chapter 21. "Lovest thou me? Feed my sheep." It's now on the cover of this book.

Today I knelt once again and prayed my prayer. I made a little list of things I wanted to do, including calls to five or six sisters who are having trouble right now— things I thought the Lord might want me to do. Then I made a even littler note of things that I would like to do if I had time.

I prayed and said, "Here's what I want to do. I feel happy with this list." And I felt the Spirit say, "That's a good list. Would you be willing to rip that list up and make a new one?"

"Well, yeeesss, but I'm not happy about it." I put it aside and made a new one. Here's my new list: give Parker a massage.

That's it. That's all. Parker is also one of those sheep. How often I forget that. He is a wonderful gift in my life who asks for very little and gives much. This reminder of how little the Lord asks, how much He gives, this reminder of how dear Parker is to me, and how simple it is to give him pleasure brings tears to my eyes. Then I turned to read my daily chapter in the scriptures.

For it is God which worketh in you both to will and to do of his good pleasure. Do all things without murmurings and disputings: That ye may be blameless and harmless, the sons of God, without rebuke ... That I may rejoice in the day of Christ ...

Philippians 2:13-16

For some reason, that answered both questions. Doing the task God has for me, no matter the result, brings the joy and peace. It isn't about the result.

I'm still working on the murmuring.

He Won't Let Us Fail
June 21st

He wants us to succeed. That's my message for the Sisters at the Visiting Teaching Conference on Saturday. Or it's God's message? I wanted to tell them to get out of their chairs and do it and quit whining about how busy they are, and they just forgot this month. As if the Sisters who succeed in doing their Visiting Teaching aren't busy! Mostly I get upset because I know how much those visits are needed. And what a blessing it is, both to those who are visited and to those who visit. *Just do it!*

But God said I couldn't say that. And I can't make them bring their Day-Timers and mark down the first day of each month as "call and set appointments" day either. That was *my* plan.

Then it occurred to me to ask God if He had a message for the sisters. I figured it was supposed to be His meeting, not mine. The title of this entry is the message He has for them. Just go to Him. He loves these sisters. They are His daughters. He loves us all. He knows what is needed and how to approach them, whether or not they come to church. Just ask Him. He'll tell us what to do. He won't let us fail.

That's my new message: He won't let us fail. Last night, I sat looking at my program and what we are presenting, and thought, *Hmm. I need more scriptures. The Scriptures bring the Holy Spirit. They are the ones that testify of Christ. I don't have enough.* I prayed/thought, "What scripture should I use to give this message?" The thought came back, *Look at the scriptures with the hymns you've chosen.*

At the corner of each page in the hymnbook are the scriptures that go with the hymn. I had chosen two hymns. "As Sisters in Zion" (*we* always sing that one) and "I'll Go Where You Want Me to Go, Dear Lord." A little twist of the knife to go along with my Just-do-it-and-quit-whining message that I don't get to give.

As I lay in bed last night, I decided to look up those hymns and the scriptures that go with them. I was tired and didn't really want to keep working on the program. But I did it. It was interesting and quick.

I thought the hymn that would have the scripture I needed would be found with "I'll Go Where You Want Me to Go, Dear Lord." But no, the Spirit said, "Look at the ones with "As Sisters in Zion." There were two. *Hmm*, I thought again. *Start with Galatians . . .* But it was no once again. "Start with D&C," the Spirit said. Ah, here it is:

> *. . . I say unto thee put your trust in that Spirit which leadeth to do good— yea, to do justly, to walk humbly, to judge righteously; and this is my Spirit. Verily, Verily I say unto you, I will impart unto you of my Spirit which shall enlighten you mind, which shall fill your soul with joy, And then shall ye know, or by this shall you know, all things whatsoever you desire of me, which are pertaining unto things of righteousness, in faith believing in me that you shall receive.*
>
> D&C 11:12-14

Perfect. By the way, here are the words to "As Sisters in Zion"—our church Relief Society's favorite song:

> *As Sisters in Zion we'll all work together*
> *The blessings of God on our labor we'll seek*
> *We'll build up his kingdom with earnest endeavor*
> *We'll comfort the weary and strengthen the weak*
>
> *The errand of angels is given to women*
> *And this is a gift that as sisters we claim*
> *To do whatsoever is gentle and human*
> *To cheer and to bless in humanity's name*
>
> *How vast is our purpose, how broad is our mission*

If we but fulfill it in spirit and deed
Oh naught but the Spirit's divinest tuition
Can give us the wisdom to truly succeed.

Emily H. Woodmansee

I guess I hadn't paid attention to those last two lines before.

P.S. I'm still working on the gentle part. I must not have been around when God was handing out that natural gentleness and kindness to the rest of the women.

The Light Dawns
June 23rd

You can't see light. I just learned that. Probably knew or had heard before, but didn't grasp on a deep level. You can't see light unless it reflects off of an object. You can't see light! This is strange. I'm completely captivated by the thought of it.

You can see the source, I suppose, if you are able to look at it without your eyes burning blind or your soul shriveling. But you can't see the light itself.

An astronaut in the book <u>The Home Planet</u> says that there is just blackness between the sun and earth—the clearest, deepest black with just pinpricks of light from far off stars – not beams of light like a flashlight. We know the light is there, because the earth reflects it. I keep looking and looking at the photograph, trying to see the beam of light between the sun and the earth. I can't. I can't see light.

I think of a flashlight. I can see *that* beam. Why? Because there are dust particles in the air, there is air itself. When we turn on a light, the room is filled with the light reflected off of the dust particles in the air. That is how we "see" that light. If the air and the dust particles weren't there, we wouldn't see light.

I am totally absorbed in this thought. I can look through light and not even know it is there, unless it is reflected. How can that which makes the material world visible be invisible?

Then I think about Christ as the "light of the world." Many don't see His light because it isn't reflected. As fewer and fewer of us reflect His light, the more people say, "There is no God."

If we want others to see it, we must reflect it.

Tripping Out
June 28th

Yes, once again we've been on the road. We just covered 3,000 miles, seven books on tape, 30 afghan rows in 3 days and are in the process of snagging two grandsons for some kid time. We'll be stopping at caves and craters on the way home. (Hanging head in shameful confession): the moms of these grandsons want me to be sure they practice reading. I plan to buy Captain Underpants™ books. Sigh. What's next? Barney?

Illuminating Prayer
July 5th

Jacob asked to be allowed to say the prayer before we headed out on Tuesday morning.

I'd been worrying about car trouble since we'd actually had a little on this trip. I was starting to think my prayers weren't working. I was filling jugs with water, since we were going across the desert on a road that sees little traffic, and worrying in my heart.

When Jacob asked to pray, and Parker said he could, I said (worried that he wouldn't pray for the key things), "Do you know what to pray for? Be sure to ask God to keep the car working, as well as for us to be safe."

In his prayer, six year old Jacob said, "And please bless

Grandma to have faith that the car will work ok."

I'm still thinking about what he actually prayed. "Please bless Grandma to have faith."

I needed that prayer. It reminds me of how powerful faith is and what a gift I have been given by God to have faith. I believe he was prompted by God to pray that prayer.

And a little child shall lead them. Isaiah 11:6

When You're Rich
July 19th

Jacob, who just finished kindergarten, is a car snob— or maybe a car expert. Anyway, he knows his cars, and he knows what he thinks of people based on their cars. He's not too impressed with our '85 Nissan.

Jacob: "What car are we driving, Grandma?"

Me: "The Nissan," watching his face become concerned. "Maybe," I say, "You could just hunker way down. That way no one will see you riding in it."

Jacob: "Yeah!" He looks relieved. Later, having decided to ride sitting straight up, he says, "Rich people can buy whatever they want."

Me: "Really? I guess that makes me rich." Jacob looks at me stunned. I watch him look around the car wondering why, if I'm rich, I drive an '85 Nissan. He looks at me questioningly. "You said if I can buy whatever I want, that makes me rich, right? And I can buy whatever I want, I must be rich."

Jacob: "But you're not really rich, huh?"

Me: "Yes I am. Because I can buy whatever I want. And you said that makes me rich."

Jacob: "You're not really rich, though, are you?"

Me: "Yes I am. Because I can buy whatever I want. The point is I don't want much. I'm happy with what I have." He just kind of laughs at me, humoring me. He's sure I'm not *really* rich.

I'm just as sure that I am.

Matthias is Missed
July 20th

Matthias moved back to Virginia last Christmas. He went to work and signed up for one class. Got a B in his first college class. Matthias has become an academic! Well, not really. But close. Paying that high, out-of-state tuition all by himself helped with the motivation, I'm sure.

His sister and aunt are putting together a special invitation, begging him to come back. Please come back. Live here. Daniel's wife Jen says to me, "How is Matthias? Will he come back here to live?"

"Do you miss him?" I ask.

"Yes," she says.

"That noise kind of grows on you, doesn't it?"

"Yes," she laughs.

He has a good heart.

The Lord's Errand
July 21st

...I do nothing of myself; but as my Father hath taught me, I speak these things. And he that sent me is with me: the Father hath not left me alone; for I do always those things that please him.

John 8:28-29

In many ways, the Lord keeps calling me to His work. I am continually reminded of the need to pray, meditate and act upon the promptings I receive. This is one of the first trips

111

during which I have taken the time to do that rather than just rushing off after a quick prayer. I have learned it is true that as I do I am not "alone, [as] I do always those things that please him".

It never occurred to me before that the Lord could shower us with feelings of his pleasure. That explains the constant joy I feel when I am acting as He wants me to.

He is pleased with us. For what? For obedience? Perhaps more for serving His children in need who often go unserved when promptings are not acted upon. When I do serve He then gives me incredible blessings. My body is filled with sweet tingles at the thought of the Lord feeling pleased with me.

An Unexpected Gift
July 25th

Home. Parker greeted me by saying he wanted to go away for two days to look at property. I said, "OK." And he said, "We'll have to go tomorrow." I laughed, sure he was joking since I just walked in the door from a two-week, 6,000-mile trip, but he wasn't.

After I'd been home only a couple of hours, we had a telephone call from Brother Mike and his wife, Carol, who called to invite us to dinner at a local restaurant. "It's all-you-can-eat spaghetti night!" they said, knowing it's my favorite. But, while we were in town returning books on tape and buying ice cream on sale, the electricity went out all over town. We could see smoke rising on the hill behind the high school. Another fire in this area that is prone to summer fires.

Sure enough the electricity was off at the restaurant, too. With nothing else to do, we went to bed. Then our electricity came back on, so we tracked down our friends and invited them to our place for all-you-could-eat spaghetti. As they were leaving much later that night, Carol said casually to me, "Did you like the quilt my mom made you?"

"Your mom made me a quilt?" I said in disbelief. Her mom made me a quilt?

"Oh!" said Parker. "I forgot to tell you. You've only been home a couple of hours. It's up on the floor near your desk." Parker forgot to tell me about a handmade quilt?

I ran upstairs with Carol following behind me, and found the quilt right where Parker said it would be. Sure enough, it was a beautiful hand-pieced quilt in an intricate pattern I'd seen her make as special gifts for members of her family. I was stunned at this gift.

"This is beautiful," I said

"It's only a single bed size," said Carol. "And it's just a summer-weight quilt, but she thought you could just use it on a couch for cool evenings."

"It's beautiful," I repeated, having a hard time believing she was just casually handing me this handmade quilt, knowing how much work it takes. I was deeply touched by this.

"She wanted to give you a gift, because you do so much for her."

I thought quickly, but could come up with *nothing* we had ever done for her. Parker and I have done a lot of things for a lot of people, but I could think of nothing we had done for her except dropped in on occasion to say hi. I said this to Carol.

"You listen to her," said Carol. "You talk with her. A lot of people ignore her. But you listen to her."

I was given a handmade quilt for listening and **talking**? Take **that**, Mrs. Bland! Mrs. Bland wrote, "Talks too much," on my fourth grade report card as if it was a bad thing and here it got me a handmade quilt. That'll show you what talking too much can get you.

I am moved by the deep wells of generosity of this woman who gave so much in return for so little.

What I Wish I'd Said
July 29th

When my children were small and wanted their ears pierced, I said, "When you're sixteen, if you still want to, you can." They did. Even the boys.

I wish I'd said, "If you still want to when you're eighteen, you can. But I hope you won't. I hope by then you'll have learned there are other not-so-permanent ways you can decorate your body. And the best jewelry you can have for your face is eyes full of love and kindness."

When my children were small and would lose their shoes, I wanted to teach them responsibility, so I said, "You lost them; you can find them. When did you last have them on? Where were you?"

I wish I'd been more concerned with teaching kindness, rather than responsibility. I wish I'd said, "Here. Let me help you. When did you last have them on? Where were you?"

When my children were small and I was busy or tired, I would ignore them or even worse, berate them. I would say, "Go away. Stop saying 'Mom, mom, mom'. Just stop whining." I wish I'd said, "Come here. Talk with me. Let me hug you."

That's what I wish I'd said.

Focus Again
August 20th

When my focus is on anything other than God is when I'm tempted to sin. We'll use the old-fashioned word here, rather than saying things like "not keep my word" or "be out of integrity" or whatever the replacement is now for "sin."

When I've been concerned with grades, I've been tempted to cheat on tests. When I'm concerned with bringing in money, I'm tempted to hold back on giving the complete truth about a product. Anytime my focus is on anything other than God, at some point I am tempted to - or will - sin. When I review my life and my shortcomings, I can see that in operation over and over.

If It's a Good Thing, Then Do It
August 22nd

I'm thinking of a comment made in a lesson in Relief Society a few weeks ago. The lesson was on "The Gift of The Holy Ghost." The teacher said, "I kept thinking I should stop and see this sister every time I passed her house. I was always in a hurry. I'd think, 'Is this the Spirit prompting me?'" She laughed to herself for a second. "And then I thought, 'Who cares if it's the Spirit or not; if it's a good thing, then do it'!"

Feed the flock of God which is among you, taking the oversight thereof, not by constraint, but willingly...
I Peter 5:2

Free Time
August 24th

The Lord has been giving me more free time. My daily task list from the Lord used to take until about 8:00 each night to finish. Lately, I've had lots of free time.

It has occurred to me more than once that the Lord is waiting to see if I've become a true servant yet or if He's going to have to keep commanding me in all things. Not that we should never have time to relax, but that I have known of unfilled needs and haven't bothered to use any of my free time to fill them.

I've been using it to read mystery novels.

I'm failing this test. I know that the Lord is chastening me, and that He is doing it for my own good.

As a man chasteneth his son, so the Lord thy God chasteneth thee.

Deuteronomy 8:5

For whom the Lord loveth he chasteneth.

Hebrews 12:6

Maybe I'm not yet ready to give up being micromanaged.

Email Q&A
August 29th

Here's an e-mail question from a teenager, the granddaughter of a minister. (I get questions like these because of our Bible-related site.) The question is:

I have been raised my entire life to believe in God and everything, and lately I have been doubting God. I have never done this before, but I have been asking myself, "How do we know that the Bible isn't made up?" I also tell myself that it is just too weird that someone can see everyone at the same time and know what they are all doing at the same time. No one knows how to help me, so I am turning to you. I've never done this before. I used to have no doubt in my mind that God was with me, but now I do. I have been praying and reading the Bible for the past few days, but nothing is working, and I don't want to lose my faith, because I was so happy before this all got into my head.

Anonymous

My reply:

There are proofs that people mentioned in the Bible actually lived, that events referred to by people in the Bible actually occurred. But this is on a broad level. I think if you are asking this question, it is because you are ready to grow your faith in God - the God the Bible tells us about. Our faith grows as we question God and turn to Him for the answers.

I know that God can see everyone, because when I pray and ask God who I can help today, I often think of a person who needs help and what help they need. When I give the help they say, "Oh thank you. I really needed that. How did you know?" Often people just need me to call and listen to them. This has happened to me so many times that I know it is God, and He knows us all and what we need.

I pray you will learn this yourself. Then you will no longer doubt God or His love for His children, especially you. Because when you see how much good your help does for others through His promptings, you realize how much He loves us all - and that includes you.

God's Will
August 30th

I used to try to be good, so that God would love me. Now I want to do good, because I know God loves me. I want to bring that same love and comfort to others. Every time I do I feel happy.

Bonuses for Readers

Audio files of the author reading sections of the book for your mp3 player or computer (a $29.97 value) Listen while you exercise or use them to share in a group or church setting.
Book club discussion guide
To get your bonuses go to
http://InHisFootsteps.com/bonuses or
http://Facebook.com/InHisFootstepsPage

12 Ways You Can Share the Book and the Message of In His Footsteps

1. Buy and share – I would be honored if you chose to buy it for yourself and for any of your friends. You can buy it online at http://InHisFootsteps.com or any local or online bookstore (Amazon or Barnes and Noble.)

2. Email – email everyone! Word-of-mouth is one of the best recommendations anyone can receive. Share what you like about In His Footsteps and where they can get it.

3. Facebook – A great place to tell friends about friends! Anything you are able to post on your wall about the book or it's message is appreciated. LIKE the page "In His Footsteps Page" at http://Facebookcom/InHisFootstepsPage

4. Bookclub – suggest In His Footsteps to your book club – your friends, your church or your online club. A discussion guide is available at http://inhisfootsteps.com/bonuses

5. Tweet – An example tweet might be "I just read "In His Footsteps from @inhisfootsteps and you should too! Order http://inhisfootsteps.com Or use hashmarks to enter the conversation #inhisfootsteps

6. Add In His Footsteps Badge – get it from http://inhisfootsteps.com/blog

7. Take the In His Footsteps Challenge - see http://inhisfootsteps.com/the-challenge and invite a friend to do it with you.

8. Blog -Do you have a blog or know someone who does? If so, consider an interview with Margaret or write about your interactions with her. You may also want to blog about particular messages from the book (the Manure Story or Thing I Wish I'd Said or one of the Wisdom prayers) and how you're using them or have had similar experiences.

9. Pictures – just for fun. Put up a picture of yourself reading In His Footsteps in an interesting place and post it on the In His Facebook Fan Page (look for the one called In His Footsteps PAGE)

10. Write a review – go to www.amazon.com or www.barnesandnoble.com and write your thoughts and favorite parts of the book. Your ideas and thoughts are always appreciated!

11. Have Margaret Speak – To your group or bookclub either in person, via a webinar or over Skype. Go to the author site MargaretAgard.com to learn more

12. Media – Interviews! Interviews! Interviews! TV, radio, newspaper, magazine, newsletters, blogs, online or offline. If you have any contacts where Margaret could be interviewed suggest they contact her at info@inhisfootsteps.com

LaVergne, TN USA
11 November 2010
204487LV00003B/18/P